T0278341

Everyone, Wherever You Are, Come One Step Closer

NAVID KERMANI

Everyone, Wherever You Are, Come One Step Closer

Questions about God

Translated by Tony Crawford

polity

Originally published in German as *Jeder soll von da, wo er ist, einen Schritt näher kommen: Fragen nach Gott* © 2022 Carl Hanser Verlag GmbH & Co. KG, Munich

This English edition © Polity Press, 2023

The translation of this book was supported by a grant from the Goethe-Institut.

Polity Press
65 Bridge Street
Cambridge CB2 1UR, UK

Polity Press
111 River Street
Hoboken, NJ 07030, USA

ISBN-13: 978-1-5095-5627-4 hardback

A catalogue record for this book is available from the British Library.

Library of Congress Control Number: 2022948538

Typeset in 11 on 14pt Warnock Pro
by Cheshire Typesetting Ltd, Cuddington, Cheshire
Printed and bound in the UK by CPI Group (UK) Ltd, Croydon

The publisher has used its best endeavours to ensure that the URLs for external websites referred to in this book are correct and active at the time of going to press. However, the publisher has no responsibility for the websites and can make no guarantee that a site will remain live or that the content is or will remain appropriate.

Every effort has been made to trace all copyright holders, but if any have been overlooked the publisher will be pleased to include any necessary credits in any subsequent reprint or edition.

For further information on Polity, visit our website:
politybooks.com

With Raha
For Ayda

The Endlessness that Surrounds Us

When your grandpa was in hospital, he asked me one night to promise him that, when he had gone from us, I would teach you Islam – our Islam: the Islam I grew up with, the Islam he too had experienced as a child in Isfahan; the Islam of our ancestors. In that dark, impersonal room, he was thinking of you.

Since then I've read aloud to you from this book and that, but none of them was what your grandpa wanted. You've learned a great deal about the Prophet and the country he was born in; about commandments and prohibitions; about scriptures, prayers, feasts and customs; about the difference between Sunnis and Shiites; you even know now about the four schools of law, and you have an idea of the problems that the Islamic world faces today. But what Islam is really about, and not just Islam, but all religions, when you get to the bottom of it – why we say we believe in God – you've learned hardly anything about that. It's as if the books were describing a person's clothes without saying a word about the person wearing them – their face, their character; not even whether it's a man or a woman, young or old; where they come from, what their dreams are, and why they love us. If religion had any deeper meaning at all in those books, it was in bringing us up to be decent people – to be just, kind, helpful and so on. But can't a person figure that out just as well, you asked, without God?

At that I stammered something about loving your neighbour, compassion, the Ten Commandments. But later, lying in bed, I thought: of course you can figure that out without God. After all, atheists are not murderers, thieves or swindlers just because they don't believe in God. And at the same time, there are so many people who do believe in God and yet are unjust, hard-hearted and cruel. So the religions must be about something more besides how we shape our lives and how we behave towards our fellow human beings. Maybe they're also, and most of all, about life itself: about what this life that we have is, and whether it consists of something more than what we see.

Some people say life is what it is: the result of chemical, molecular and genetic processes, a kind of supercomputer that is constantly developing itself by trial and error, adaptation and selection, cause and effect. Grandpa always pointed out that someone must have built and programmed this computer that makes everything tick. And when others insisted, no, there is no one who builds and programs life; it comes about by itself and disappears again like a drop of water that evaporates and dissolves into thin air – then Grandpa always said something that is cannot simply become nothing: neither a drop of water nor a human being nor the fact that we exist. And he claimed, furthermore, that the idea that something could become nothing is almost impossible for children to conceive of. And do you know what? I think your grandpa was right about that.

It is interesting, after all, that children, if I'm not mistaken, practically never question the meaning of life – don't even dwell on it much, while adults certainly do. Oh yes, and how they question and dwell! So there must be something between being a child and being an adult that shakes our belief that everything is just as it should be. Try to remember when you were a little child: did you use to think a lot, about death for example, when you were younger? I don't think you did, really. You knew that we all die someday, but it wasn't something you thought about; to you it seemed as though life would just go on somehow. You weren't afraid at all; on the contrary – when I talked about the afterlife, about Heaven, angels and eternal life, it was the most natural thing in the world to you. You simply couldn't imagine that something that is could suddenly not be, from one breath to the next.

Only now that your own grandpa has died, and you've grown older yourself – at twelve you're almost a teenager – have you met death face to face. You wept at his grave. You noticed something was wrong; Grandpa is gone; he'll never tell you a story again; you'll never go visit him by the seaside in summer. Maybe you've thought for the first time about the fact that you too will lie in the ground one day, in one of those cold, clammy graves. That we all will turn to dust: your mother, your father, your sister. And I think this *conscious* confrontation with death is one of the things that happens between being a child and being an adult. It doesn't have to be a certain person who dies; what I mean is simply the clear realization that someday we won't be around any more, none of us. And two, three or at most four generations after us, there won't be anyone left around who remembers us either.

> Know that earthly life is but a game
> And an amusement and a frippery and a contest,
> Who is the richest, who has the most children.
> It is as rain that makes the plants sprout,
> And makes the whole village glad.
> Then they wither, and you see them turn yellow and dry.
> And everything decays.
>
> Surah 57:20

Of course, our great- or great-great- or great-great-great-grandchildren will know we existed – otherwise they wouldn't exist. But who we are, what we think, feel, dream, what makes us feel concerned, angry, glad, afraid or excited: they won't have the slightest clue about that. We'll just be gone, as if erased; not even our names will be known; even the inscription on our tombstone will weather and become illegible, no more recognizable than our faces in old photos. All the people we loved, and we ourselves too, will evaporate like a drop of water – into nothing, it seems.

Sooner or later each of us realizes with a chill that nothing of us will last. Then we begin to doubt: does life really go on somehow when a person dies, as our parents always said? And where was I before I was born? Sooner or later, every human being wonders about questions like these, and their answers differ vastly. But perhaps it is not the adults who know best with their long and their short explanations, but the children, who trust that life will go on somehow and everything is as it should be. And the Quran – and all revelations, for that matter – confirm what children think. They say, just look around you – do you really think all this can be just by chance?

> Look at the water you drink –
> Did you send it down from the clouds, or did We?
> If We wanted, We could make it bitter.
> Why then do you not give thanks?
> Look at the fire you have kindled –
> Did you create the wood, or did We?
> We created it as a reminder
> And to serve those who cross the desert.
> Therefore praise the name of your Lord Who is almighty.
>
> Surah 56:68ff.

And yesterday, as my gaze strayed out of the window while we were reading another book about Islam, I suddenly thought there is more to learn about God out there, or at least more important things than the fact that the Quran contains

114 surahs and what the first, second, third, fourth and fifth pillars of Islam are. After all, Islam and Christianity and Judaism and all the other religions were not created in offices, in libraries or in classrooms. The religions came into being wherever people looked around at nature, or worried about their loved ones when they themselves were sick, hungry or feeling lost, when their children were born or when their parents died – at the most important events there are in a person's life. And why? Because they noticed they were surrounded by endlessness. Yes, endlessness. The sky, for example, up there, if you look out of the window right now – not the Earth's atmosphere, I mean, but the universe, space – does it have an end? No, of course not. But can you imagine that something just goes on, goes on and on forever? Think about what that means. You'll find that you can't imagine endlessness.

Or take the chestnut tree in the yard – yes, that one: can you conceive that out of trillions and quadrillions of leaves that have sprouted since the world began, not a single one is the same as another? I mean, not only each one of that tree's leaves is different from every other, even if you could lay every leaf the tree ever grew side by side – but all the leaves of all the trees of all time: not a single leaf that ever grew or ever will grow is the same as any other. And there you have another endlessness, an endless diversity this time – one that you can see but can't explain, much less produce yourself. But this amazement, the amazement at all the things, occurrences and phenomena in the world, which you can see but can't explain because they exceed our limited understanding – some of them frightening, many amazingly beautiful – precisely this amazement is the origin of Islam, and of all religions. Because all of us, your grandparents, your parents, you, your sister, and one day your children and grandchildren, all of us are born and eventually die. Just like the leaves of the chestnut tree in the courtyard, and like every creature on Earth, we flourish and wilt. Not even the stones, the lifeless, unremarkable pebbles lying around in the yard, have always existed, nor will they always exist. Something must have existed before the stones, before the buildings, streets, churches of our city, before the huts and the paths, before the people who settled here; some kind of field I suppose, a ploughed field, and before the fields, the riverbank was lined with meadows and bushes, or the land was covered with primeval forests. But the meadows and forests weren't always there either, nor even the river. Before that, perhaps there was ice, or maybe just rocks; maybe this was all a sea at one time. In any case, even the rocks came into being only gradually; they formed over thousands or millions of years, and in thousands or millions of years more, there will be nothing left of them. Not even the rocks! In other words, everything that exists is finite; it begins, and at some point it ends. But the sky – the sky never ends.

When the Earth no longer exists, there will still be the sky, whether there are stars in it then or not. And there is no limit to the diversity of shapes that a leaf can take either. Even if the world were to go on existing for millions and millions of years, Nature would still find a new shape for every single leaf of every single tree – just as it does for the face, the hands, the toes, the fingertips and the eyelashes, if you like, of every single person who ever lived or ever will live. Nothing is the same as anything else, absolutely nothing – not even eyelashes! That's what I meant when I said we are surrounded by endlessness.

And that is where religion arises: it is a relationship between the finite beings that we are and the infinite, which is also called God. And that is the subject of the book I want to write – no, I have to write: the book I promised your grandpa shortly before he died. We'll write it together, rather: every evening I'll read you the notes I've made while you're in school, and the next day I'll start with your questions and objections. And maybe it won't be a book just about Islam, but about what's common to all religions. We'll see where you lead us.

And in Our Selves

Okay, you're right: if no hand is the same as another, you said yesterday, then we're endless too. Or, to put it more precisely, although we are mortal, we too are part of an infinite diversity. On the spur of the moment I couldn't think of a rebuttal, but this morning, while I was brushing my teeth, I thought: each of us, every living thing, carries something endless in ourselves. You could also say that is the divine in us. But, at the same time, every one of us, and likewise every leaf on the chestnut tree in the courtyard, has a beginning and an end: we are born and we die, we grow and decay. This finiteness is the terrestrial in us. That means every person, and every creature of any kind, carries in itself the relationship between the infinite and the finite. Or, in other words, the divine is not something external, but lies in ourselves. We are mortal and hence human, but in our uniqueness – yes, precisely by the fact that we are unique and unmistakable and unrepeatable – we are part of an endless diversity, and hence divine.

That sounds a little bit like inspirational Sunday radio, I'm afraid. And yet it's actually physics – quantum physics, in fact. Quantum physics studies the tiniest building blocks of matter – molecules, atoms and much smaller elementary particles, millions of times smaller than anything we can see with the naked eye. So small it makes even physicists woozy.

Because, actually, physics is the study of what we call reality. The word 'reality' comes from the Latin *res*, which means 'a matter' or 'a thing'. I can take a thing in my hand – an apple, let's say – and that's reality. The apple in my hand is real. God, on the other hand, would be an assertion that you either believe in or don't: in other words, religion.

But it's not as simple as that; at least, not in Islam. And not in physics either. Because physics has discovered that these tiniest building blocks of existence don't exist – not in the ordinary sense of the word at least, as something with clear boundaries, much less something you could put your finger on. In other words, not only in outer space or on other planets, not only in science fiction or religion – no, in each one of us, too, there is a reality that is different from everything we know.

On Earth are signs for the sure in faith
And in yourselves – do you not see?
Surah 51:20-1

That other, inner reality obeys other laws; it has a different structure from our reality; we can't call it what it is with the words we have. In that reality, particles are in different places at the same time; they react to each other no matter how far apart they are; they can jump from one place to another without passing through the space in between. And nothing can be predicted by exact calculations, because the principle of cause and effect doesn't always apply. It's a reality without 'matter' or 'things'.

God, as your grandpa explained Him to me, is not so very different. Strictly speaking, Grandpa didn't believe in God at all: he saw God, he grasped God – really, the way you grasp something with your hand; he smelled God – the way you see, *grasp*, smell an apple. Indeed, by saying 'God', Grandpa created Him, in a sense: that is, he gave an expression to that which exists only for itself, just as the apple only becomes 'an apple' in your mind. The apple is already there, but it has no name; it doesn't belong to any category of fruits; it just exists – no, it 'functions'; it grows from a bud, ripens in the sun, becomes food for an animal or falls to the earth, to which it returns as it gradually decomposes. It is human beings who give this reality a name which is distinct from those of other realities: apple. Not tree, not pear, not hand. And, in Islam, God – this is perhaps the most important thing of all that your grandpa tried to teach me, and my grandparents thought the same – in Islam, God is just as real as an apple, or a breath of wind or, you could also say, a feeling such as love or fear. Only different from all the things we know. Not a person, not an animal, not a fantasy.

Okay, what then? you will probably ask. What is He like, this God, and where, and how come? And yet, you yourself phrased it very similarly yesterday evening – all right, you didn't talk about quantum physics, but you did mention an essential principle of it when you said we too, although we are finite, are nonetheless part of infinity. I'll try to explain that – but I'm warning you, it's going to get a bit complicated. If you've had enough of physics already, just bring back your mind at the end of the 'Extra Section'.

Extra Section on Spirit and Quantum Physics!

Imagine you're looking closer and closer at an object – let's say one of the leaves of the chestnut tree – up close first, then with a magnifying glass, then under a microscope, and so on: you divide the leaf into tiny parts and split one of those parts again, and again; first a cell, then a molecule, until you get to the atoms, but then you split one of the atoms into its parts, and then you come to the subatomic particles, the electrons, neutrons and protons.

And, for every particle, there is an anti-particle with the opposite charge, and they can change into one another or release energy when they collide. Then they cancel each other out, and emit two light particles, photons, in their place. If you keep on looking closer, you'll find that the subatomic particles are made of quarks, which are connected to other quarks as if by an invisible thread, and between them . . . is nothing: no body, only an oscillation, energy, interaction or potential.

Those are fuzzy words, I know, but not even quantum physics, the most precise of all the sciences, has unambiguous words for it – because the phenomenon itself is ambiguous. For quantum physics has discovered – and this was perhaps the greatest scientific revolution of the twentieth century, on which all of today's technologies are based, not only atomic energy, but also computers, lasers, magnetic resonance tomography, solar energy and the Internet, down to your smartphone – quantum physics has discovered that our existence, at its core, is not matter, something material, but something else, something unnameable which is actually not 'matter' and not a 'thing' – a reality without a *res*. Because words refer to concepts, which means something that you can grasp, or feel, or at least circumscribe. Words work in a world of either–or: either it's the apple, or it's the hand holding the apple.

But if you keep splitting an object into its component parts (better the apple than the hand!), and keep splitting and splitting, in the end there is no object left, only something that you can't explain, define, grasp with your mind; at most you can only observe it, describe it, and be amazed at it.

For example, physicists discovered that the same subatomic particle – something much smaller than an atom – behaves like an object, and at the same time like a wave. That's not possible, the quantum physicist's brain thought. But the measurements showed that something can be its opposite at the same time: an object and a non-object. It is beyond our words and concepts – but it exists. Yes, and what's more: ultimately, only this One, Indivisible, Immaterial exists, and all life develops from it, just as a single cell becomes many by cell division – except that this One isn't a cell, but something more airy, more of the nature of a process.

Airy, I said just now. The word is not so poorly chosen, since even rigorous quantum physics sometimes can't find a better word for this One Thing than 'spirit'. One of the founders of quantum theory, Werner Heisenberg, even said once that the Greek philosopher Plato was quite right: the real world is that of forms, and we can see only shadows of it. And Heisenberg's daughter Christine reported that her father's eyes glowed with joy as he spoke, like the eyes of a child receiving a huge present. This world, Heisenberg attested time after time, this inner world that holds all the outwardly graspable things together is so unbelievably beautiful that it takes your breath away.

Beauty – I thought that was something you can see or hear or smell. Not something abstract, something thought up; not just empty space. And spirit is first of all formless, and thus unbounded, but at the same time it is associated with a certain being, or sometimes with a group or an era. The Arabic and Persian languages, and also Greek, English and the Indian languages, frame this contrast clearly: for *ruḥ*, *nafs*, *pneuma*, *spirit* and *atman* all go back to the sense of 'breath' or 'puff of wind'. This seems to be a general awareness among humanity: that breathing is not just the most elementary activity of every person, but the fundamental principle of life itself. You still have some of this knowledge in the biblical German word *Odem*, which is related to the modern word *Atem*: God breathed His *Odem* into Man, that is, He breathed His spirit into him, He breathed life into him.

'Spirit' in this sense is thus not only something spiritual, immaterial, but at the same time something physically perceptible, tangible, like air. And the critical thing is – you brought it to my attention yesterday – that all of us are part of this same One that contains so many possibilities. Whenever you draw a breath, you're connected with the whole world. Every time you breathe out, the world receives part of you.

End of the Extra Section on Spirit and Quantum Physics!

So 'spirit' or 'breath' would be a second metaphor for God, after endlessness which I talked about yesterday. After all, human beings didn't always have microscopes, much less the ability to split atoms. But they have always felt the air filling up their chest, rising and falling, invisible, inexplicable, and yet real. The most important thing of all in life, the most personal, and at the same time something that exists in every creature – and you have no power over it! You can hold your breath if you want, but afterwards you'll exhale all the more vigorously. Neither were you able to control your first breath, nor will you have any power over your last breath. You are completely dependent on an external power, a 'spirit', that awakens you with your first breath, and sustains you a long time, I hope, before it takes your life back again. And this principle – that human beings must gasp for air because by nature they want to live, no matter how unpleasant and difficult their existence may be – this principle is present everywhere in nature.

People saw the plants and animals all around growing and decaying, the sun and the moon, the earth and the seas giving them food and taking all the bodies after their death, and they felt – from the beginning of time people felt that the world is not put together out of independent parts, but that there is a common fundamental principle at work in everything: 'the breath of the All-merciful', as the world is called in Islam. Yes, the whole of Creation is the 'breath of the All-merciful'. For Grandpa, this fundamental principle existed, this oneness, the *tawḥīd*, just as undoubtedly as in physics something exists beyond or before or between our world of objects. Except that, in religion, you don't need a laboratory; a look out the window or a single breath tells you enough. God is not something you just believe in; God is something you see if you look closely.

> Don't pursue what you know nothing about;
> For it is the ears, eyes, heart
> Which shall be called to account.

Surah 17:36

By the way, about your smartphone: how do you explain the fact that you just have to press a couple of buttons and you're connected with Aunt Jaleh in Iran? Telephones used to be connected by wires, sure, and I once read you a story about the first cable being laid between Europe and America in the nineteenth century, by two ships sailing towards each other – what a sensation that was in those days. Maybe I'm a bit old-fashioned, but I always thought that today, instead of a cable, there was some kind of antenna, and this antenna sends out some kind of vibrations, and they cause another vibration, and so the vibrations go out across the ether to a satellite, and from the satellite back down again to Aunt Jaleh's phone, something like waves on the ocean. Only recently I learned that there is no ether. That is, the waves have no material medium; there's nothing there to vibrate, not even the thinnest air. It's as if waves rolled across an ocean although there was no water. And yet Aunt Jaleh's phone rings in Isfahan. Would God then be the ocean that isn't there, or the wave that nonetheless travels from one shore to the other? Or both, or nothing? Think about that.

Your grandpa was not a physicist, but as a doctor he had a scientific view of the human body, and likewise of nature in general. I'm sure he himself treated many people in the hospital who were beyond curing: he knew the constantly growing capabilities of medicine, and the limits that it will never overcome. There is a strange sentence he always said, and that his grandpa had probably said too, and his grandpa and *his* grandpa, and all our grandmas and great-grandmas too: 'Hold on tight to God's rope.' God is everything, and hence eternal and unlimited. But His breath is very specific. God is both.

Yes, I Testify

Oh my God – if I'd known you were going to get so enthusiastic about quantum physics, I wouldn't have said anything about it. Because now you're pestering me with questions about force fields, probability waves and the quantization of energy. Am I Stephen Hawking? If only I'd stuck to the Quran! Then you wouldn't be asking me about the miracles; you would have accepted them as natural, as in any other story. You're right: a smartphone is a technical device that can be explained and built. But for Jesus to be born without a biological father, walk on water or wake the dead will always be inexplicable – if it really happened at all.

Now I could make the excuse that that's the Christians' problem: after all, Jesus is their Messiah, not ours. Fortunately for your common sense, and my parental duty, Muhammad never performed any supernatural feats. But that wouldn't get me far, because you would rightly point out that Islam explicitly recognizes Jesus' miracles.

All right, I could still say those miracle stories were meant only metaphorically. The virgin birth, for example, would be the Bible's way of saying that Jesus was sent by God, and not the product of a man's semen. But that might be taking an easy way out; in any case, your next objection would inevitably be: then why is Jesus the product of a woman's egg?

Well, instead of pursuing what I know nothing about (Surah 17:36 from yesterday!), let's read Surah 19, starting at verse 16, where the Quran tells about Mary's pregnancy.

> And in the Book recall Mary
> When she went away from her people
> Towards the East
> And hid herself.
> We sent to her Our spirit [literally, 'breath', 'puff of air'!]
> Which appeared before her as a well-formed human being.
> 'I take refuge before you in the All-merciful', she cried,
> 'Maybe you fear Him.'
> 'I am a messenger of your Lord', he said,
> 'To bestow on you a good son.'
> 'How can I have a boy', she asked,
> 'When no man has touched me,
> And I am not a whore?'
> The spirit said, 'Thus says your Lord to you:
> "That is easy for Me;
> And so We will make the child a sign to the people,
> And a mercy from Us.
> The matter is decided."'
> She conceived him
> And went with him to a place far away.

Now don't shout right away that the whole thing about the virgin birth is complete nonsense. Try at least to understand the difference between this version and the Christian story. There will still be time to tell me I'm off my rocker. The difference is that, in an Islamic concept of the world, Mary's pregnancy is not a miracle in the way we think of miracles today – as something supernatural. In the Quran, Mary's pregnancy is no more unusual than nature itself. That's why your grandpa, who otherwise saw everything so rationally and scientifically, was never much amazed at Jesus not having a biological father. Why should he be? he said, when he heard how Christians today discuss the idea; he was much more amazed at the discussion! Because the sense of the Quran is, rather, that if we look only for superficial causes and effects, and don't take the spiritual world into account, our understanding of reality just isn't deep enough. The universe too is an indisputable physical fact, and we can investigate it scientifically and trace it back to the Big Bang. But we will never understand why the world began if we search for the reasons only within the world.

> See, to God, Jesus is the same as Adam:
> He created him from earth, and then He said to him,
> 'Be!' and he was.
>   *Surah* 3:59

Still not convinced? Just wait; you'll live to see much bigger miracles. No, you already have: starting with your own birth. You could retrace every effect to every possible cause, back to the beginning of time theoretically, and never find the reason why there exists something rather than nothing. Maybe the virgin birth is really only a picture, a story, a metaphor; but you yourself, your eyes, your nose, your belly, your laugh that makes me laugh too every time, no matter how sad I may be – you exist. In Islam, both the virgin birth and life itself stand for this same inexplicability: we see something and can't possibly deny it, and although our rational mind is not sufficient to discover its cause, that doesn't imply at all that the cause doesn't exist.

Now maybe you'll say people didn't yet understand the cause in those days, but today we're further along; we can explain why a person comes into being, from fertilization to mitosis – cell division – to birth. In that case, I'll ask you: but why is there cell division; why are there cells; why are there atoms? If I keep on asking, I always come to a point where even science runs out of answers. Science, I would claim, can't even explain the love that draws two people together to conceive a child like you.

It's no wonder that the proportion of people who believe in God is much higher among physicists and mathematicians, who deal with unimaginable things day in and day out in the course of their research, than among sociologists or psychologists. Yes, there are studies! And if you doubt me again, google it yourself. Almost all of the pioneers of quantum physics in particular found their way to religion sooner or later, although it wasn't always Christianity, Judaism or any specific denomination. 'That deeply emotional conviction of the presence of a superior reasoning power, which is revealed in the incomprehensible universe, forms my idea of God', said Albert Einstein. Einstein believed in God, not although he was a scientist, but *because* he was a scientist. In other words, to him, science and faith, rationality and spirituality, complemented each other. 'The cosmic religious experience is the strongest and noblest mainspring of scientific research.'

I know it is still unusual, eighty years after Einstein, to think of science and religion together. In your school, the two subjects are kept strictly separate, I assume – Religious Education being classified, rather, under ethics or philosophy. And a miracle, colloquially, is something you believe, or don't as the case may be: a miracle violates the laws of physics. In Islam, on the other hand, those laws that you perceive behind all phenomena are themselves the miracle. There is a reason for everything in this Creation, absolutely everything, however tiny and insignificant every single living thing may be individually, and even for the most unusual, arbitrary, randomly acting, astounding thing. For every single one of us.

And the mountains that you think are immovable,
You shall see passing as the clouds:

The work of God, Who has ordered every thing.
And He is aware of what you do.

$Surah$ 27:88

Why do you suppose I'm a Muslim? Sure, I'm a Muslim
because my parents and my ancestors were Muslims and set
me an example, encouraged me, trained me in Islam. If I had
been born in a Christian household, I would very probably be a
Christian today. When you look at it that way, it was by chance
that I became a Muslim. Just as it is by chance that your father
isn't encouraging you to become a Buddhist, for example.

I could have decided against Islam at some point, however.
The Quran emphasizes over and over again that faith must be
based on your own experience, your own thinking, your own
insight. Among the five roots or principles of faith, the *uṣūl*,
which are much more important to us than the famous five
pillars, *arkān*, that your school's explanation of Islam makes
so much of – among the five principles, many Muslims count
Reason (*'aql*) third, right after the Unity of God (*tawḥīd*) and
the Prophecy (*nubūwa*), but before Justice (*'adl*) and belief in
the Resurrection (*ma'ād*). That's why in Islam a person is supposed to choose the religion consciously only when they are
13, 14 years old – that is, when they reach the age of consent.
Surah 2, verse 170, goes as far as to explicitly criticize people
who blindly follow the belief of their fathers: 'But what if their
fathers didn't understand anything?'

Every day there are stories in the news that reflect poorly on
Islam. In Iran, where we come from, the people are oppressed
in the name of Islam. In the Quran itself, I come across verses
that alarm me. Why then have I not turned away from Islam?
Why am I – although I have travelled so much and visited
countries where the conception of Islam is narrow-minded
and even violent, although I have read so many books, on other
religions as well as Islam – why have I, in full knowledge of the
facts, remained a Muslim?

This part is going to be more complicated – or, come to think of it, maybe not. I am a Muslim because I can say the profession of faith, the *shahāda*: There is no God but God, and Muhammad is His prophet. If you agree with these two statements, you are a Muslim, and no one may cast doubt on your faith; no one has the right to ask you anything else about it, or to contend that you're a bad Muslim. Everything else, the five principles of faith, the five pillars, the prohibitions and commandments – they are important; they are recommended; but they do not determine whether you are a Muslim or not.

There is no God but God, and Muhammad is His prophet: the first affirmation concerns God; the second, human beings' relationship to God – that is, religion. The first affirmation says that the same power is at work in all phenomena: beyond the duality – or, to put it more exactly, *in* the duality – by which we are obliged to comprehend reality. In all of the diversity and inconsistency of life, there is a unity that connects everything with everything: something inseparable and creative. That is what is meant by the affirmation that there is no God but God: no other cause, only this one creative force; in all phenomena, the same principle of the *tawḥīd* is at work, the unity of God. And the second affirmation says that this one creative power, everywhere the same, reveals itself to us in all the diversity of the Earth and the stars, people and peoples, if we only look close enough – that God makes Himself heard. For if I recognize Muhammad, I recognize at the same time in Islam all the other prophets who were sent before him.

Do you follow me?

The power that produces everything not only exists, but you can recognize it: this dual idea is what the profession of faith expresses.

Now I have been calling it a profession of faith, but that's actually not the right term at all. To profess is in fact a very Christian concept. Strictly speaking, the word *shahāda*, which is translated as 'profession of faith', means 'testimony', in the sense of 'bearing witness': 'I testify that there is no God but God.' Testimony, profession of faith – the distinction seems minor, and yet it says a great deal about how Muslims see the world. For professing means declaring that you belong to a specific doctrine or a specific group; it is always a profession *of* something or standing *for* something. Christians profess Christianity – that is, they believe in it. Or I may profess that I am a fan of FC Cologne, or that I love Schubert. I can profess my affiliation only if it would be equally possible to profess a different one, such as Real Madrid or Taylor Swift.

Testimony is different: testimony is based on an observation – one which, objectively, may be ambiguous, but to you personally is as clear as the apple you're holding in your hand. A quantum physicist testifies that the tiniest building blocks of matter are not material. I testify that a certain Schubert sonata has touched my heart. If you were honest for once, you would testify that I'm a better Monopoly player than you – yes, I am! 'Am I not your Lord?' God asks the human beings on the day of their creation in Surah 7:172. 'Yes, we testify', the people answer. And God explicitly says that they are giving testimony; they are witnesses stating facts in court:

> We take you as witnesses
> Lest you should say on the Day of Resurrection,
> 'We were not aware of this!'

Professing means: among different alternatives, I profess my choice of this particular one. Testifying, on the other hand, means that you have seen or experienced something. The alternative to that is not some other testimony – what you have witnessed is too clear for that (my winning streak at Monopoly, for example); the alternative to testifying is denying the obvious (for example, claiming that you're actually a much better player and I'm just lucky). Accordingly, in the Quran, the unbelievers do not have the wrong belief among several possible beliefs. No: like you when you deny my outstanding skills at Monopoly, the unbelievers are 'deaf, mute and blind – hence they do not understand', as the Quran phrases it time after time. And 'they do not understand', *lā ya'qilūna*, actually means here they do not perceive, do not take in with their senses, and thus do not recognize. 'And among them are some who listen to you', God says to the Prophet in Surah 10:42, talking about the unbelievers, and I'm going to rub your nose in this the next time you lose:

> But can you speak to the deaf,
> Though they do not understand?
> And among them someone looks at you;
> But can you show something to the blind,
> Though they see nothing?

The faithful, on the other hand, are, in the Quran, those who do the obvious: namely, see, hear, smell, feel, recognize that the same power is at work behind all phenomena, in every single heart:

> Your God is a single God;
> No god is there but He,
> The Merciful, the Compassionate.

> See, in the creation of heaven and earth
> And the alternation of night and day
> And the ships that sail the sea
> For people's benefit
> And the water that God sends down from the sky
> With which He revives the Earth after its death,
> And the animals of all kinds that He scatters upon it,
> And the winds that blow this way and that,

And the clouds which serve between heaven and earth:
See, there are signs for people of reason.

Surah 2:163f.

The problem with religion is not that it's so complicated. The problem is that it is so simple. We think and think and think, and don't understand at all, or we forget while we're thinking that the main thing is completely obvious. No, I don't mean my winning at Monopoly – although, that too, of course.

Remember the word 'spirit': it sounded so lofty, so abstract; and yet, as we saw, it originally means nothing but 'breath' or 'puff of air' – the most natural occurrence in the world. Try it yourself: inhale deeply and hold your breath – you feel pressure in your chest; breathe out again, and you immediately feel released. And yet breathing, with all its difference, duality and reversal, is just that puff of air. It's that simple, that basic, that tangible: in breathing, in the very fact of breathing, is all of life with all its contradictions: compulsion and freedom; pain and joy; chance and predetermination; constriction and release.

And we can take it further: the next time you're alone, concentrate only on your breathing for ten or, let's say, twenty minutes – you'll see how it gradually takes you away from the everyday reality surrounding you. It's a little bit like falling asleep: that transition from waking to dreaming. And every now and again you lose your sense of time. That's exactly how meditation works: at the beginning, you have a thousand images and ideas fluttering through your head, but with some patience and practice – the third, fourth, or maybe not until the tenth time – the mental playlist gradually comes to a halt, and your thoughts run out. Fulfilment – this is another paradox – fulfilment doesn't mean having a lot in you, but having very little. Because then your soul becomes a vessel.

Probably all the religions teach that, when we breathe, something divine flows in us, or that with every breath the world spirit – that is, what connects all creatures together – mixes

with your soul. In the Quran, Islam is also defined as 'expanding your chest': that is, as inhaling. When you speak the first
word of our prayer, the word *allāh* in the Arabic intonation,
dwelling on the extended consonant 'l', which is articulated
not in the usual way at the front of your mouth, but with your
tongue almost on your palate, creating a deep resonance that
you can feel down to your belly – each time, it is as though this
breath or this spirit of God trembles in you for two or three
seconds before it flows back into the world with the initially
deep, then steadily rising, 'a': *alllllloaaaaaah.*

Scholars have so many theories about where the word 'Allah'
comes from, what it originally meant, whether the Muslims
use it differently from the Arab Christians, whether 'Allah' is a
proper name or simply the Arabic word for 'God'. But nowhere
have I read the explanation that *alllllloaaaaaah* just sounds
absolutely wonderful and sets off this deep resonance in your
body, which is a religious practice in itself. It's no coincidence
that the Indian word for 'soul', *om*, which Buddhists and
Hindus repeat in meditation, resonates in the same chamber:
om too is that kind of 'expanding your chest'. These are magic
words, and there are two or three of them in every religious
tradition: they not only mean something, but they also create
a mood all by themselves that transports you away from day-
to-day life. It can also be a sequence of words, as in the rosary
that many Christians pray, or a certain body movement, like
the salute to the sun in yoga.

And that brings me back to the first – the simple – answer to
your question why I'm a Muslim. Of course, Islam is a clearly
defined religion with certain rules, beliefs, doctrines and so
forth. But, at the same time, the basic principles of Islam are
so simple that you can find them – in different words, with
different rules, by different prophets – in almost every other
religion, and also among the indigenous peoples. You could
say they are universal. That's why the Quran says every person
is born a Muslim: not because they heard of Muhammad in

their mother's womb, but because human beings, before they learn any doctrines or concepts at all, possesses a natural religiousness. That, fundamentally, is what Islam is to me. In the end, the distinction between 'profession of faith' or 'testimony', between Christianity and Islam, is not that great. A Christian too feels and sees; a Muslim too has no evidence to give that would be admissible in any earthly court.

Yes, I am a Muslim because I was born in a Muslim household. But I became a Muslim because God can be found in any other house too. 'Everybody, wherever you are, come one step closer', says a little story that I discovered in my own grandpa's memoirs. The story actually comes from an old Persian book, and it's a true story:

> Once, when Sheikh Abū Saʿīd, one of the most famous Islamic mystics of the eleventh century, came to Tous, a city that now lies in north-eastern Iran, so many of the faithful streamed into the mosque to hear him preach that there was no more room for those still arriving. 'May God forgive me,' cried the usher, 'everybody, wherever you are, come one step closer.' Then the sheikh ended the assembly before it had begun. 'The usher has already said everything that I wanted to say, and what all the prophets have said', he explained, before turning around and leaving the city: 'Everybody, wherever you are, come one step closer.'

In a Relationship

That was a proper question you asked yesterday evening: what does Islam actually mean? Because, as a writer, I know a thing or two about language and literature. To be exact, you meant it as an objection – as usual – not a question: whether a person 'professes' or 'testifies' something doesn't make a great difference. The crucial thing is, *what* do they testify or profess? That's what I should have started with – what is Islam? – instead of some linguistic analysis.

In my defence, I can start by pointing out that it almost always helps to understand the literal meaning of an expression or a name, because that often gives a clue to its deeper meaning. Judaism and Hinduism, for example, are both derived from the names of certain peoples: the Jews and the Hindus; the deeper meaning of both terms is a certain human community's relationship to God, or, since the community in question stands for all communities, you could also say humanity's relationship to God. Meanwhile, Christianity, Buddhism and some almost forgotten religions such as Manichaeism and Zoroastrianism are named after a person: Jesus or Buddha, Mani or Zarathustra. These faiths are centred not on the community, but on an individual person, or on 'the individual' in general.

Of course, in all religions you find both relationships to God: that of the community and that of the individual. But each religion emphasizes certain important aspects – such as the one we talked about yesterday: whether a person 'professes belief' in God or 'attests' to God's existence – and only all the religions taken together give you a complete picture. They are not mutually exclusive, but they are not the same either; ideally, they complement each other precisely because of their differences. Just as we people do, and we peoples; or as different scientific theories do, if you like.

Imagine, for example, you decide later on to study physics. You'd have lectures on the general theory of relativity in the morning, and on quantum mechanics in the afternoon. What would you think? You'd think the professors didn't have both oars in the water, or else they hadn't spoken to one another in a century. Because the concepts of the world that they're teaching you are completely contradictory: in the morning, the world is a curved space in which everything can be calculated, in principle, billions of years in advance; and in the afternoon, the world changes into a flat space in which quanta of energy jump around like mad, and not even the next second is predictable. The crazy thing is that both theories work incredibly well. Nature, explains the physicist I am indebted to for this example, is to us like the old rabbi two men called upon to settle a dispute. The rabbi listened to the first man, and said, 'You're right.' Then he listened to the other man, and said, 'You're also right.' Then the rabbi's wife yelled from the next room, 'But they can't both be right!' The rabbi thought for a long time, and then said to his wife, 'You're right too.'

In Islam, as in other religions, there is an original community with a specific language, and there is one particular person who points the way to God. And yet our religion is not named after the Arabs, nor after the Prophet Muhammad; instead it is named – like Chinese Taoism, the only other such case – after what is *between* God and humankind: after the relationship. Because 'Islam' is derived from the word for 'peace', *salām* in Arabic, or *shalom* in Hebrew, and means to submit, to surrender, to make peace.

All right, those are three different meanings (and I could add more possible translations of *'islām*), but there's nothing so unusual about that. In English too, there are many words that are ambiguous, and whose meaning only becomes clear in the given context. 'Love', for example – to take the first one that comes to mind – 'love' can mean all kinds of things, from liking something, when you say you looove spaghetti ice cream, to feelings of tenderness, to such an uncontrollable physical desire that two people fall upon each other as if they wanted to devour each other. Some words even have meanings that are completely unrelated, and not just poetic words such as 'love' or 'goodness', but ordinary everyday words.

If I know you, you're going to demand an example of such a word too, before you believe me.

So take, let's say, the word 'serve': I serve your lunch the minute you get home from school – that is, I bring it to the table; or perhaps I serve you: I have no ambitions of my own, but do whatever you command. I could also serve at tennis, but that just means it's my turn to hit the ball first. And so on and so forth.

Language is rarely unambiguous, and it is important to keep that in the back of your mind when you read the Quran, and likewise when you read the Bible or any other scripture revealed by God. Yes, especially if you read the Quran or the Bible, because the Quran consists, in Arabic, of rhymed verses from beginning to end, like a poem, and the Bible consists of narrative, like a storybook. But poems and stories always have more than just one sense, because their language is so mysterious and beautiful that every reader can find a different meaning in them.

God has sent down the most beautiful pronouncement,
A book, resembling and repeating itself,
From which the skin shivers of those
Who fear their Lord;
Then their skin softens,
Their heart remembers God.

Surah 39:23

With laws or traffic lights, on the other hand, beauty doesn't enter into it: what matters is for everyone to understand the same meaning; otherwise, no one would be safe from theft, or all the cars would start across a junction at the same time – thou shalt not steal, the red light means stop, full stop. With a poem or a story, this full stop is never reached: a poem has different meanings even to the same person when we hear it a second, third, fourth time. You could also say that poetry, or the domain of art in general, is governed by that freedom that we can't permit ourselves in everyday life, because there it would infringe on other people's freedom. The imagination is unlimited, which makes it our most divine faculty.

Now you'll want another example, I suppose.

You and your examples! All right. Say, today you read *Lisa and Lottie*, about three years after the first time you read it, and you discover a lot of details you didn't notice then. Or today you decide *Lisa and Lottie* is boring, although three years ago it was your favourite book. Yet not a word of the book has changed! You're the one who has changed; you're reading the same pages with new eyes. Or let's take a piano sonata by Franz Schubert, to bring in my favourite music: to one person, the famous beginning of the first Impromptu, with its sparse, hesitant notes, sounds very sad, like a parting, or like death itself. Others hear the opening more as a promising start, a cautious but joyful beginning, like the first buds opening after a long winter. And to still other listeners, the first Impromptu seems so tender that they feel they can hear in it the love of another person – in the same few notes! You can try this experiment yourself: play the beginning of the first Impromptu for three people and ask them what mood the music evokes – I'll bet you a spaghetti ice cream sundae that you'll get three different answers. And I'll bet you a whole ice cream parlour that the same sonata sounds different depending on whether you yourself are sad or happy at the moment.

Why is that? I think it's because every work of art, every piece of music, every poem is a mirror in which you see yourself – but a mirror made of a thousand little mirrors, differently curved, sometimes tinted, round, angled, oval, so that your gaze is reflected differently, or the reflection is strangely distorted, with every tiny movement. And the same thing is true when you read the Quran or the Bible, which are both much more complex than *Lisa and Lottie*: they have ellipses, images, riddles; they're actually composed like music, with rhythms and sounds – you won't find two people who read the same thing in a surah of the Quran or a book of the Bible, as long as they approach it with curiosity, an open mind and their own questions. And that's exactly how it should be; exactly that is the richness of the holy scriptures, and of all poetry and literature for that matter: that they have more than one meaning, and every time you read them you can discover new aspects of the same truth – an infinite number of aspects, which brings us back again to the endlessness all around us. So if someday somebody tells you this verse of the Quran or that story from the Bible means this or that, you can be sure that other meanings are equally possible. The Quran is a book between two covers and does not speak, said Imam Ali, the first, or for some Muslims the third, successor of the Prophet – it is people who make the Quran speak. But people are all different: every single one is different from everyone else, especially in different times, countries, climates; and one and the same Quran will shine in so many different ways in their readings.

What do I mean by that?

Well, suppose you were angry and looking for a fight: then you'd find passages in the Quran that reinforce your anger. But if you're in a conciliatory mood, just the Arabic sounds of the Quran will feel to you like gentleness itself. Or your mood may change; that could happen too: you're spoiling for a fight, and the Quran makes you think of an idea that pacifies you, or gives you a feeling, reminds you of something, starts you daydreaming – but the idea, the feeling, the memory or the daydream, they didn't exist anywhere else but in you. A philosopher reads the Quran as theory; a poet is inspired by its allegories, its rhythm, its language. A democrat reads the Quran as a manifesto for freedom; a dictator feels it means him when it talks about God. The wife-beater appeals to the Quran, and the woman fighting for her rights strikes back with the Quran. One and the same book, first recited 1,400 years ago in Mecca, reveals in each person what they carry in their heart – but rarely notice. People think they are following the Quran when the Quran is only amplifying the voice they already have within themselves. And if that voice rants, rages and barks, their disposition must not be a friendly one. The Islam I'm trying to explain to you has, I admit, a great deal to do with the person I've turned out to be, not least thanks to my parents. And what you find in Islam will likewise be a reflection of your own soul, along with all your influences.

Because that's what matters deep down – in all the teachings of wisdom, in all the religions; that's the founding precept of philosophy too: 'Know thyself.' The truth is not written somewhere in books: you find it in yourself, hidden under all the opinions, lies, egoisms, urges, fears, wishes, self-images, all the rehashed and blindly ingested teachings that wrap themselves like vines around your consciousness while you're growing up. 'The kingdom of God is within you', Jesus taught, and Muhammad said it not very differently: 'He who knows himself knows his Lord.' The books, the prophets, the poets, and the sciences too, and hopefully your parents, teachers, models, and all the verses of the Quran, are only signposts to yourself.

And, since I mentioned Taoism earlier: *Tao* means simply 'the way'. There just can't be a more beautiful name for a religion. In that sense, the sheikh we talked about yesterday, Sheikh Abu Sa'id, was surely a Taoist.

But if that's so, if the holy scriptures do not supply the answer, but only help in the search, then neither the Bible nor the Quran, and much less the Tao Te Ching, can be left to speak for itself. You can't just google what God says in it about this or that. It is in the nature of the Torah – the five books of Moses, to Jews the holiest part of the Bible – that it needed the Mishnah, the commentary, from the beginning. And in every classical Quran commentary, it is customary for the scholar to begin by listing all the other interpretations of a given verse: 'It is said, verse such and such means . . .; it is also said the verse means . . .; it is also said that the verse . . .; it is also said . . .'; and so on . . . five, six, sometimes ten different interpretations of the same verse before the scholar finally dares to give his own interpretation: 'But I say the verse means . . .'. And at the end of every such interpretation of any verse in every classical Quran commentary comes the phrase *wa-llāhu a'lam*: 'And God knows better.'

But don't think that part, at least, is free of ambiguity. Far from it! Not even this final, invariable formula that follows every explanation of every verse of the Quran is perfectly clear, because *wa-llāhu a'lam* can also mean 'And God knows best' – a tiny difference, you may think, and yet this alone can fill whole libraries with possible explanations! And because God unites opposites in Himself, just as nature does, you can probably find the story of the rabbi that I just told you in every other religion, in one form or another. In Islam, it goes like this:

Umar ibn al-Khattab said: I heard Hisham recite the surah *Al-Furqān* differently from how the Messenger of God taught it to me. I wanted to scold him, but I waited until he had finished reciting it. Then I grabbed him by the neck and took him to the Messenger of God and said, 'O Messenger of God, I heard this man recite the surah *Al-Furqān* differently from how you taught it to me.'

The Messenger of God bade me let go of Hisham, and then told him to recite it. So Hisham recited the Quran just as I had heard him do.

'Thus it was revealed', said the Messenger of God.

Then he told me to recite it.

When I had done so, the Messenger of God said again, 'Thus it was revealed. The Quran was revealed in seven ways. So recite it whichever way is easiest for you.'

Okay, the Islamic version doesn't have the rabbi's wife, who brings the humour into the story. But, on the other hand, here it's the Prophet himself who declares different readings of the Quran equally valid. The number seven is always understood as a token for 'infinitely many', as in the references to 'seven Heavens' in many cultures: what they mean is that Heaven is endless. And so the Quran was revealed in endless different ways.

God's immutable word and the different human interpretations of it go together seamlessly, and one reason for the whole mess that Islam is in today is that most of our scholars have lost the living, and thus changing, relationship to the Quran. Quite a few of them only parrot what the scholars before them wrote – and not just ten or twenty years before them, but back in the Middle Ages. We're seeing the consequences in the Islamic world today, many centuries later: backwardness, poverty, irrationality, an atrophied sense of humour, fundamentalism, violence, misogyny and so on. Such a dry, petrified Islam, unchanged for a thousand years and now nearly dead, has nothing more to say in a world in which not only quantum physics but, after many wars and genocides, human rights too have finally been discovered. And yet Muslims could find a foundation in the Quran both for modern science and for political justice – although they would have to apply their minds and their creativity. Because the Quran praises reason, and it pronounces all human beings equal. If religions are a way, then Islam too cannot be unchanging.

Of course, you can find exceptions and glimmers of hope: among young people in particular, you can find a will to see Islam with new eyes. But, so far, our religion is still such a sorry, dreadful sight that I'm sometimes ashamed to belong to it. Your grandpa felt, at the end of his life, it was all the more important to communicate and pass on to you that religion is actually something beautiful, something that helps and enriches your life – that God loves us. Because you belong to a new generation which, I hope, will find a new understanding of Islam and, with every reading of the Quran, every reflection, every action, remember the highest commandment of Islam: compassion, which the Quran mentions no less than 600 times.

> Herein is indeed a message for a people who serve.
> We sent you only out of compassion for all the world.
>> Surah 21:106f.

But that's not what I wanted to talk about now. I'll talk about the infinity of meanings when I tell you a little about the Quran and how God speaks to us human beings: namely, not as a policeman – do this, do that – but as a great poet or storyteller – 'God tells the best stories', says Surah 12, verse 3. For now, though, I just want to note that the very word 'Islam' is not at all as straightforward as it appears at first glance. 'Submitting' is a different act from 'surrendering' or 'making peace' – think about each of the different meanings. And yet there is something all three words have in common. In all three translations, the word 'Islam' stands for a relationship: a Muslim is a person who submits to someone, who surrenders to someone, who makes peace with someone.

But who is the someone? I'll try to answer that tomorrow; I've already talked more than I intended to today: you'll be home from school any minute and will want something to eat. I'm afraid I can't feed your stomach with religious instruction. Islam is important, but so is pasta with tomato sauce.

Something Bigger than Us

I admit that was a rather flippant remark – about the pasta, I mean. But there is a grain of truth in it. Of course we can only think about religion when we have time for it, opportunity, leisure. A hungry person, a person going mad with thirst, a person in fear of death or – the reverse – in extreme ecstasy doesn't think about God. They only think about what is troubling them, or delighting them.

That is in contradiction to what I wrote the first day, I notice just now. Then, I claimed that religions began with the fundamental experiences of every life. Now I see I need to be more precise. Religions start the moment we think about those experiences: when we're amazed, when we look for an explanation or when we feel helpless. Religions start, not with the experience itself, but with the questions it raises. And then people always find new answers, which they call truths; that's perfectly normal, and all kinds of answers taken together make a religion, which is called Islam or Christianity or Buddhism. Sometimes there are also disputes among the religions, or they declare war on one another. And do you know why? Then you can tell me this evening, because I don't know.

But to come back to the word 'Islam': the name means a very specific relationship between human beings and – who, exactly? God, of course, a theologian or an academic would say: a Muslim is someone who enters into a certain relationship with God. God is a very abstract term, however. We can't imagine God very well, because He is different from everything we know: He has no nose, no mouth – He has no form at all. How can we imagine something that doesn't look like anything? That's why I suggest we leave the word 'God' aside for now and go back to the endlessness that surrounds us. Although endlessness is also impossible to imagine, at least you have it right before your eyes when you look up at the sky, at a leaf of the chestnut tree, or in the face of a human being: all the lines, for example, the contours, colours, the porous surface, on which there are thousands, hundreds of thousands, or infinitely many details to discover.

And if you now take the word 'Islam' – just its three literal meanings, 'submitting', 'surrendering' or 'making peace' – that brings you pretty close to the core of our faith. Because a Muslim is a person who, recognizing their own human limitations, submits to the endlessness. But a person who, in love and fascination, surrenders to the endlessness – during a hike in the wilderness for example, or when they die and go into the unknown – is also a Muslim. And so is someone who makes peace with the fact that they are surrounded by endlessness, and doesn't constantly rebel against the inexplicable. In other words, a Muslim lives in harmony with the infinite, affirming it and acknowledging that it is bigger than we are: *allāhu akbar*, as the muezzin calls from the minaret, with that mysterious quavering on the second 'a', pronounced long and low: *allāāāhu akbar!*

Allāhu akbar doesn't mean 'God is great', as it is often translated. 'Great', 'large' or 'big' in Arabic is *kabīr*: to say that, the muezzin would have to call *allāhu kabīr*. *Akbar* is the elative form of *kabīr*, used as a comparative, and means 'bigger'. But *akbar* is also used for the superlative, and then it means 'the biggest'. Besides the fact that *allāāāhu akbar*, with the same vowel pronounced short, long and short again in succession, sounds much more beautiful than *allāhu kabīr* – the meaning too is richer, and at the same time more exact, I think. 'God is big' doesn't mean anything, actually: how big, then? As big as a house, a tower, an ocean? Ultimately, God would still have some worldly dimensions.

But when the muezzin calls *allāhu akbar*, he means that God exceeds all human and earthly dimensions: 'God is greater' (to stick with the comparative sense of *akbar*), just as endlessness exceeds all measurement. But a thing can be greater only in comparison with something else, and that brings you right back to the relationship that the word 'Islam' indicates: the relationship of human beings (and also animals, and all creatures) to something that is bigger, stronger, older than themselves; the relationship to that which has always existed and always will exist; that is, the relationship to the endlessness, to use our provisional metaphor for God. Or you could say, instead of endlessness, our relationship to the universe, to nature, or to the origin from which all creatures come.

Now you're going to object – I can see it coming; when we get to this point this evening, you're going to say it's perfectly obvious that human beings realize their own limitations and their dependency. Yes, I'll answer you in advance; yes, at least, we're born with the awareness that there is something bigger than ourselves: in the beginning, our mother, naturally, whose breast feeds us; our father, who protects us. Of course, that's not adequately gendered today, but let's not think about today: think of the conditions of life over the millennia, when mothers and fathers naturally had different functions for their baby. I said before that religions arose not in schoolrooms, but from the fundamental, truly existential experiences, and if we call God a father, and some believers quite rightly call God a mother, they don't mean that God is a man or a woman.

They mean that the relationship is similar to those. And if the relationships are different today, then the image human beings have of God will gradually change too, and then God too may well become non-binary.

Babies know intuitively that their parents are there to love, feed and protect them, and they cry out for them whenever they feel uncomfortable. They know that there is something bigger on which they are dependent. And they learn that, when their mother goes away, she comes back again. No mother is always there, just as God, later, will not always be there. The crucial experience is that the baby's mother always comes back. The confidence that babies gradually acquire is the foundation for our later trust in God. Now maybe you can understand better why Jesus says we should learn faith from children. Like children, we too are supposed to trust that God is there even when we don't see Him.

But then children grow up and grow stronger and more self-assured, while their parents grow weak and infirm, and at some point it may happen that a person thinks there is nothing bigger than them after all, and they aren't dependent on anyone. In the worst case, the person becomes a tyrant and thinks the world revolves around him. Yet all a person has to do is look up in the sky, or at the tree outside their window, to know: neither they nor any other human being will ever be able to create any of it so perfectly, not a single leaf of a tree; and their life, their happiness, is not under their control – not even their own heart. A person may grow as rich as they like, may become powerful, build fifteen skyscrapers, conquer whole continents or own half the world like Jeff Bezos – when their heart, from one second to the next, stops beating, it is of no use. And if his child's heart were to stop beating, even Jeff Bezos would be nothing but a miserable wretch.

The submission, the surrender or the peace that are contained in the word 'Islam' mean exactly that realization, and also the acceptance that we stand, with every breath, in relation to something that is stronger, more powerful and also more beautiful than we – God is closer to you than your own jugular vein, says Surah 50, verse 16. We feel hurt, we die and turn to dust, and nevertheless everything is as it should be, even though we often don't understand it – especially the hurt. That's what I meant when I said Islam, to me, means to live in harmony with the universe which surrounds us, and of which we are a tiny part.

Say: 'O God, Lord of everything!
You give lordship to whomever You will,
And take the lordship from whomever You will.
You raise up whom You will,
And cast down whom You will;
In Your hand goodness lies.
You have power over all things.
You make the night turn into day
And make the day turn into night.
You bring forth the living from the dead.
And bring forth the dead from the living;
You give to whom You will without measure.

Surah 3:26f.

Words like 'power' and 'submission' sound rather uncomfortable today, I won't try to deny it. Does that make them wrong? The universe, or nature or fate, can in fact be pretty uncomfortable. Fate can bring accidents, tsunamis, nuclear meltdowns and wars; illnesses too, of course; sorrow and grief; and yet many people still believe in God. Life doesn't work according to our plans and, by the same token, we can't put together a God to please ourselves. No, we have to take God as He shows Himself to us, and if God produces all the wonderful things – flowers, love, food, imagination – then, since He is everything, or the universe, the unfortunate things must have something to do with Him too: injustice, poverty, natural disasters and pandemics, atomic bombs, all the despair in the world. It feels good to say God loves us, and yet the religions teach us that God can also inflict terror.

Suppose you're having a fight with your sister, or you're really cross with me, let's say, because I'm scolding you although you haven't done anything, so I'm treating you unjustly: you'd be angry; you'd slam the door – and yet you wouldn't stop loving your sister for one second, nor me either, I hope. I'm not saying siblings never grow apart as they get older, or that children never disown their parents. But it's no coincidence that the Bible says we should learn faith from children – that is, take their instinctive reactions, feelings, mentalities, their sense of wonder and their enthusiasm as our guideline. And yet you can't imagine, I suppose, that your love for your sister or your parents could ever fall apart, or even diminish. Least of all is parental love, which is most like God's love, subject to conditions or dependent on a child's actions.

God is everything, and even though we don't always under-stand Him, we still believe in Him, make peace with the world, surrender to His love, accept His power, fear His violence and, yes, we submit, too. And that does not make us as helpless as it may sound at first, because it also means we submit only to this higher power, to the infinite, and not to some other person – that is, not to our parents and not to our teachers, and certainly not to a president or king. When everything is about power, money, recognition, it can be truly liberating to believe in something higher, something that is not measurable by the standards of this world, something that urges us in fact to make sacrifices rather than think of our own benefit. Such a faith gives you a deep equanimity, because you no longer think everything is under your control. To the believer, this earthly life is little more than a transient state anyway, a kind of transit lounge that you're welcome to enjoy; you have to work hard sometimes, but on the whole you don't have to take it all too seriously – no more seriously than literature, and that's something a writer takes seriously indeed!

Or, since you're not so interested in poetry, let me try to explain it another way. Imagine you're travelling: you're not as upset about a water leak at your holiday rental as you would be if you had damp walls in your own home, where you're going to live all your life. Nonetheless, as a good guest, you take care of the rental flat and inform the owner so that the next guests won't have water dripping on their heads.

> Let there be no compulsion in religion;
> The right path is clear from the wrong.
> Whoever repudiates idols and believes in God
> Has gripped the firm handhold which never breaks.
>
> Surah 2:256

Besides, the submission to God is done voluntarily; you could also decide against Him: 'Let there be no compulsion in religion.' Hence the translation of the word 'Islam' would be incomplete if it didn't also include surrender – surrender to someone or something that you love – as well as peace, which you make in your heart. Because the crucial aspect of this relationship is, 'He loves them, and they love Him', as Surah 5, verse 54, has it, or the New Testament, more concisely: 'God *is* love.' That is, we are not simply dependent on this eternal power that created us and gives us warmth, food, beauty; we are not only grateful and love the Infinite – no: conversely, the Creator also loves His Creation. Your grandpa always used to say, that's beautiful, knowing that: God loves us as a mother loves her child, or a man his wife, or the sun the flowers.

But the sun can't love! I said to him – I was as old as you are now.

How do you know that? Grandpa asked me; how did I know whether love is what we human beings think it is? Maybe love is warming, feeding and touching another without asking for anything in return. Or turning to someone and reaching out to them wherever they come into view. Just as the sun turns to the flower, God turns to us and embraces us with His light. And just as we turn towards God, the flower turns towards the sun when it comes up on the horizon, and misses it at night, or when the sky is covered with clouds.

I don't know if that's right. Sometimes, when I despair at the injustice on earth, the poverty, the wars, the mischief that we human beings commit against one another, and against Creation, I think it's all rubbish. Then I remember your grandpa; I see him lying in the hospital. He had grown so wan; the pain tormented him, and he was no doubt worrying about us, his children, and probably still more about his grandchildren and great-grandchildren: what would become of them on this earth that humanity is in the process of destroying? Would it really happen as God is warning us it will? Because no matter what havoc human beings wreak, even if they spark a nuclear war, it won't be the end of life on Earth – only the end of our species. Nature will survive us and go on evolving without humanity.

> O, do you not see that God in truth
> Created Heaven and Earth?
> If He will, He can take you away
> And bring forth a new Creation.
> ### Surah 14:19

Grandpa worried most of all about Grandma, who would be left behind alone, old and frail, and I am sure he was also afraid, afraid of death. But then we saw how his fear grew less and less. How his confidence returned: that very childish trust, you might say, that everything will be all right in the end – when he dies, that is. And that trust gave him peace; you saw that in him in his last days. And peace is the root meaning of the three consonants s–l–m from which the word Islam is formed. But *salām* or *shalom* is also what the Christians wish their dead when they say 'rest in peace'. Peace is what lay in Grandpa's face when he was finally released from the pain.

What do you think: where is Grandpa's soul now?

Black Light

So, you think it's nonsense that the sun and the flowers love each other? You call that sentimental tripe? And it doesn't help if I point out that love, in the context of nature, isn't necessarily used in the literal sense, as when people love each other, but describes something more like . . . positive energy, or will to live, symbiosis, attraction?

Humph.

I'll try another way. You know the Creation story – how God created the world in seven days. Obviously, the book called Genesis doesn't minutely describe the sequence of events from the Big Bang to the pinnacle of Creation, which is now sitting before you in the form of your father (and which is not fond of being told it's talking sentimental tripe). The Bible and the Quran are not science textbooks; they tell about Creation in the form of a story. I know what you're going to ask this evening: why didn't God just tell it like it was? Why didn't he bring Moses up to date, or at least Muhammad?

And you can guess what I'm going to answer: the answer is contained in the question itself. Whatever scientific explanations the Bible or the Quran could have adduced – they would only have been 'up to date' as of 2,600 years ago, when the Creation chapter in the Bible very probably originated, or 1,400 years ago, when Muhammad recited the Quran in Mecca. Because scientific implies human, and human knowledge is always developing. Two thousand six hundred years ago, people simply wouldn't have had the prerequisites to understand a theory of today, and in 2,600 years from now, quantum physics will surely have become obsolete in its turn. God doesn't talk to us like a scientist; He speaks to us like a poet. The meanings of language are finite, because it consists of discrete words with definite boundaries, but in poetry, language opens up towards the infinite.

> And if all the trees on Earth were pens,
> The sea ink for them, and seven seas after it,
> Never the words of God would be exhausted.
> Behold, God is mighty and wise.
>   Surah 31:27

Unlike every scientific theory, a story – a good story – is universal: even if it was first told thousands of years ago, it is nonetheless applicable to any time and any continent. A story also keeps pace with scientific knowledge. Two thousand six hundred years ago, no one would have understood the term 'Big Bang', if only because explosions were very rare occurrences before the Machine Age; at best, people would have thought of a thunderstorm or a volcanic eruption, and if you had claimed that the Earth wasn't the centre of the universe, even Aristotle would have cried Hogwash!

But such a splendid biblical phrase as 'God said: Let there be light! and there was light', or in the Quran, where God says, still more concisely: '"Be!" and it is' (kun fa-yakūn) – peasants in Judaea were able to set such a phrase in relation to their world, and it will still have meaning to astrophysicists in a future colony on Mars, who probably won't look up at the sky any more except through a digital lens. The peasants would have thought of a seed planted in the earth; the astrophysicists would think of a signal received by their telescope. But both of them form an image of the world's creation, its development, in accordance with its own immutable laws, after an initial event – the Big Bang if you like, in which the primordial matter, with infinite density and infinite heat, is supposed to have exploded within a fraction of a second – until the solar system finally came about, some 9 billion years later. That, more or less, is the first day in Genesis, which is followed by God's creation of the heavens, the earth, and human beings in five more extremely condensed and wonderfully mysterious chapters: from the light of the sun to the creation of water to the formation of dry land, the germination of plants, the creation of animals, the development of human beings; and on the seventh day, God rested.

And before all that?

Well, before that there must have been something or someone too, I think – before the Big Bang, I mean: a single, indeterminate being, a nothing, a spirit, a will, that created life out of the primordial matter within a fraction of a second – shorter than the word 'be!' or the Arabic *kun!* It may well be that science will never find out what caused the Big Bang. But, up until a few centuries ago, all people believed, even far away from all civilizations, on the remotest island, in the deepest jungles, in the middle of the desert, in something like God. That belief seems to be intrinsic in human beings, or in Creation itself:

To God is the course of life.

Surah 24:42

Now the relationship that is contained in the word 'Islam', like any relationship, involves at least two persons: not just God, but also a human being. Or God and all human beings – that is, humankind. Or you could also say, Creator and creature, because in Islam, in Christianity, in Judaism, not only human beings are in a relationship with God, but all living beings, including the animals and plants.

> The seven heavens and the earth praise Him,
> And whoever is in them –
> There is nothing that does not extol His praise.
>
> *Surah 17:44*

Not only does the Quran mention many kinds of animals, but some surahs are named after animals, such as 'The Cow', 'The Ant' and 'The Bee'. In contrast to what we find in the Bible, in which Man is supposed to subdue the earth, the animals' purpose in the Quran is not to be used by us human beings. No: the animals have a right to exist in themselves; they will be called forth at Judgement Day alongside human beings; they are even called 'nations' just as we are:

> There is no creature crawling on the earth, nor no bird
> That flies on its wings,
> Which are not nations like you.
> We have passed over nothing in the Book;
> All will be gathered before their Lord.
>
> *Surah 6:38*

The rocks too? I asked your grandpa; and the sun? The sea? In other words, the non-living parts of nature?

Grandpa wasn't sure. Later, I discovered that the Quran doesn't explicitly mention the souls of rocks or the sun and the sea, and that we human beings have to figure out a lot of things for ourselves, if God tells us about the 13.8 billion years from the Big Bang to the first life on Earth in just a few verses. All animals have a relationship to God: okay – does that include the microbes? When do we call something a living being? An animal? When do we call something a human being – from which month of gestation? All that is left undefined. And then, suddenly, even the ants are supposed to have a relationship to God, a loving relationship at that – how does that work?

There are lots of stories about how the saints were careful when they walked to avoid hurting even an ant, because the ants too are sacred creatures of God. When Imam Ali, the son-in-law and successor of the Prophet, accidently stepped on an ant and hurt it, he was so upset that he wept as he tried to set the ant back on its feet. At night he dreamt he heard the Prophet accusing him: he ought to have been more careful where he walked; all Heaven had been sorrowful for two days on account of the ant, while the ant, for its part, was busy praising God. The Imam began to tremble all over, and a cold sweat broke out on his brow, until finally the Prophet comforted him: the ant itself had interceded for him with God.

You can find such respect for animals, sometimes bordering on the comical, in other religions too. Francis of Assisi talked to the animals as close friends, and in India, among the Hindus, some sadhus – religious ascetics – walk only with a broom before them so they don't step on any ants. I admit you're not likely to become world champion in the 100 metres that way – but the world champion of hearts, maybe! Of ant hearts, at least. But many human beings too have loved and continue to love these saints, who showed more respect, more love, greater surrender before Creation than we are able to do in our day-to-day lives.

Now please don't ask me this evening whether ants even have hearts, and what their relationship to God looks like. That's a question for a biologist. Biologists, or scientists in general, have a lot to say about religion because they observe and explore nature more closely than we do. And there is certainly a reason why astronauts and quantum physicists, in particular – not all, but a striking number of them – so often mention God, and they're the people with the broadest overview and the people with the most microscopic eye.

I've done a little research in the meantime so I won't look stupid next time you ask me about nature. And, because you seem to be more impressed by scientific findings than by poetic verses – what could your writer father have done to deserve that? – I'm just going to quote the most respected scholars for the rest of this chapter. Because – guess what I've noticed – in the end, even science waxes poetic. For example, I was reading a book of texts by all kinds of astronauts, who described their impressions on seeing the Earth from space for the first time. 'What took no analysis [. . .] no microscopic examination, no laborious processing, was the overwhelming beauty . . . the stark contrast between bright colourful home and stark black infinity', one of them recalled, 'the unavoidable and awesome personal relationship, suddenly realized, with all life on this planet . . . Earth, our home.'

When you look up from below, you have an inkling that everything is interconnected, but you're seeing it from the perspective of the particular. But the astronauts see all the particulars from the perspective of the whole. Researchers now have a technical name for the awe that inevitably overcomes them: it's called the Overview Effect. 'The first day or so we all pointed to our countries', a Saudi astronaut recounts. 'The third or fourth day we were pointing to our continents. By the fifth day, we were aware of only one Earth.' That is exactly analogous to the visions of Muhammad or the Italian poet Dante Alighieri, the dream journeys of Muslim and many other saints through the cosmos: in each case, the experience of travelling in the heavens replaces particularity with wholeness – the realization that everything is connected to everything else and you are a part of something bigger. In meditation, that is experienced as a rising up and out, comparable with the astronauts' rising out of Earth's gravity, a rising out of the individual earthly existence: all at once, the mystic is blessed with a view of things from above, and sees himself or herself, not as the central point, but as an integral part of the whole world. A Russian cosmonaut describes the shift in perspective still more exactly:

> When we look into the sky it seems to us to be endless. We breathe without thinking about it, as is natural. We think without consideration about the boundless ocean of air, and then you sit aboard a spacecraft, you tear away from Earth, and within ten minutes you have been carried straight through the layer of air, and beyond there is nothing! The 'boundless' blue sky, the ocean which gives us breath and protects us from endless black and death, is but an infinitesimally thin film.

What does 'infinitesimally' mean? Don't worry, I had to look it up too.

'Infinitesimal' is a term from mathematics, and means 'becoming infinitely small, approaching zero'. Something like what happens in quantum physics, which I've also read up on to be ready to stand your test: you look closer and closer – your perspective changes in the opposite direction from space travel – and yet the resulting impression is evidently quite similar. What's more, the findings made in the world of elementary particles are completely compatible with the findings over the tremendous distances of the cosmos – even though the data are based on different, practically opposite methods, and the two scientific communities work completely independently of each other. Even the physicists, the most precise natural scientists of all, struggle time and again to keep their composure when they discover an incredible, superhuman order in every single phenomenon, however chaotic it seems from outside. 'Physical research has established as an incontestable fact that these basic building blocks of the Universe do not exist unrelated in isolated groups, but that all of them are mutually interlinked according to one uniform plan', wrote Max Planck, whose name you may know from the news, since one of the most important scientific research associations in Germany is named after him. 'In other words, every process in nature is subject to a universal and up to a point knowable law.'

'An incontestable fact', Planck writes. Not all scientists would subscribe to that and, if you look, you will find staunch atheists among the quantum physicists as well. I didn't quote the sentence to prove God exists, because there is no proof of God. I quoted it to explain Islam, which also points to nature as the strongest indication of a divine dispensation. And because I can't go for long without verse, I'd like to quote the Quran – forgive me – one more time before I go make lunch:

> Behold, in the creation of Heaven and Earth
> And the alternation of night and day
> Are indeed signs for insightful people.
> Standing, sitting, lying,
> They remember God and reflect
> On Heaven and Earth which are Creation:
> 'Our Lord! You have not created this in vain!
> Praise be to You!'
> Surah 3:190f.

When it began, Islamic theology for this reason wasn't – just one more thing I have to say before I go cook – wasn't a religious doctrine at all. It was counted as one of the sciences, alongside mathematics, astronomy and physics. And many, if not most, of the great religious scholars and philosophers of the early times were at the same time scientists, physicians or astronomers – in the Middle East just as in India, ancient Greece and China. And, present-day prejudices notwithstanding, religion and science are not opposites: in Christianity too, natural science was for a long time a part of theology. The very researchers we have to thank for our modern concept of the world and our technical progress – Johannes Kepler, Isaac Newton and even Galileo Galilei, who was hauled up in front of the Inquisition in Rome in 1632 – all of them were highly educated in theology, and deeply religious. They only rejected their church's obsolete dogmas – or, rather, it took a few hundred years before the church finally had to admit they were right. Yet it was precisely their belief in the rationality of the structure of the cosmos, and hence in God the Creator, that gave Kepler, Newton and Galileo the strength, the unflagging curiosity and the inexhaustible patience to continue unravelling the laws of the celestial spheres for years, decades, under extreme hardship, in complete isolation and against the resistance of the authorities of the time.

Do you remember the amazement that I told you about in the first chapter – the amazement at all the things, phenomena and events in the world that you see but can't explain because they exceed our limited rational faculties, some of them frightening, many wondrously beautiful? That amazement, I said, is the beginning of religion. But it is also the beginning of science. Scientists search for the forces that move the cosmos and are amazed, surprised, awestruck to discover their regularity. Mystics discover in themselves, in their breathing or in their feelings on contemplating a flower or listening to music, in their dreams and visions on bringing their thoughts to a stop so that their subconscious becomes visible, down to the buried memories of birth and security – mystics discover in their own soul the very same laws, and the same polarities, that keep nature in balance. But I, when I'm in the woods or in the garden, simply kneel down as I used to do when I was a child to look at the bees, spellbound at how they do their work, divide up their tasks, fly so purposefully from here to there, as if they never had a moment's doubt about anything. Who explained all the different crisscrossing paths, to all of them at once, so that they never get in each other's way? And they are performing an invaluable, indispensable service to all the other creatures in the forest. Then I get an inkling – no, I feel it as concretely as you feel a breeze or heat or a touch – that there

is an order in everything, and a creative power at work in the
bees themselves, and even in the microbes.

> And your Lord prompted the bee:
> 'Look in the mountains for homes and in the trees,
> In the houses and in the cities,
> Then eat of all kinds of fruit
> And follow the easy paths of your Lord.'
> Out of their bodies comes a drink,
> Various in colour,
> Which contains a physic for human beings.
> Indeed, therein is a sign for those who reflect.
>
> Surah 16:68f.

But know it, the way you know that two and two are four or
that school starts at eight tomorrow morning? No, I don't know
it, of course, because, as a practical matter, bees sting when I
touch them, and microbes are much too small to see with the
naked eye. I could use a microscope, but even for the strongest
lens in the world there would be particles – smaller than atoms
or molecules – so small that a scientist can only infer that they
are there. And, by the same token, even the cognitive powers
of physicists and the imagination of the astronauts are limited,
and there will always be things that we just can't imagine – the
soul, for example, or the centre of the earth, or your beating
me at Monopoly one day. Ah, that already happened again
last week? Then imagine something yourself that you can't
imagine.

Naturally, that's nonsense: you can't imagine something
that you can't imagine. And yet the sentence is true, as self-
contradictory as it is; as a paradox – where have you heard
that word lately? Think back to quantum physics again: that
also involved phenomena, in the innermost core of our existence, for which there are no words in our everyday language.
That's nothing new; people have always had a feeling that not

only God is a poet, but human beings too can talk about the highest truths only in poetic language: that is, in allegories, through sounds, and also, and indeed mainly, in paradoxes – in sentences that are actually illogical. Why? Because the highest truths are beyond the grasp of our reason. They are bigger than we are. And among all the instruments of poetry, paradox is often the best suited to say something that can't be said in an ordinary, correct sentence.

Good God, now I suppose you'll want an example again. You and your examples!

Okay, I'll give you one of my favourite paradoxes: black light. Some mystics – that is, people looking for God within themselves – have talked about seeing in their meditation a black light shining. There is no such thing as a black light, of course; it's logically impossible: blackness is the opposite of light. And yet the phrase immediately gives you the idea of a radiance that is different from everything that is humanly known. You can close your own eyes, and if you concentrate long enough, you'll notice that inside your eyelids is not simply darkness, but something else, something hard to define. And that is exactly how the mystics described the experience of God: it was like a black light.

Now I hope my knowledge of astronomy, quantum physics and space exploration has impressed you enough to make you willing to bear the greatest hardships: I haven't cooked anything, and you're already at the door. May the celestial spheres lend you sufficient strength, unbounded patience with me and insatiable yearning for . . . a sandwich.

Short and Sweet

Okay, fine, thank you very much. You're still not convinced by my explanation of why God speaks in images, instead of just telling Moses or Muhammad how the Creation went? You think, if God is all-powerful and all-knowing, He would have been able to phrase the scientifically correct version of the Creation story so that both a peasant in Judaea and an astrophysicist on Mars would understand it equally well, and all doubts would have been done away with for all time? It's wonderful that you know all the answers – maybe you could give God a few pointers. And the slight damper it would have put on our thirst for knowledge if humankind had known everything right from the start, that wouldn't bother you either, right? Mastering fire, for example; inventing the wheel or discovering the theory of relativity – human beings didn't need curiosity for that, you say. The question is just why God didn't offer Adam and Eve a course in astrophysics, based on the latest science of, let's say, the year 5023; then everything would have been settled at least until then. Oh, that's right, Adam and Eve are just a metaphor. I suggest you put in for the job of prophet yourself.

You know, the whole problem with my book is that it

consists of a lot of explanations. I try to describe something that is inherently indescribable, at least in the language we use in day-to-day life – in understandable terms, logical reasoning, simple sentences. That's the fundamental problem of theology, the 'study of God' (or of gods): it teaches something that, strictly speaking, can't be taught. In some religions, God must not even be named, since His reality is so different from anything that can be said in words. And yet theology has to try to find explanations, interpretations, arguments; and we would be more ignorant if we didn't think about religion and try to rationalize our relationship to the Infinite – that is, to classify it, draw implications from it, penetrate the Bible and the Quran with the tools of science, philology, archaeology, comparative phenomenology of religion, historical research, literary scholarship and so on; when you listen to music, let's say Schubert's first Impromptu, it's helpful and it enriches your mind to find out how the individual notes are formed, where the inconspicuous repetitions are hidden, and how the different variations are interrelated. It also helps to learn something about Schubert's time, about his illness, about his love, which was of course ill-starred.

Yet, as necessary as theology is, it just as necessarily fails again and again, or has to admit its limitations. Ultimately, I can't put into words why exactly the first Impromptu goes straight to my heart every time I hear it, and the same is true of God: ultimately, language can only approach the ineffable from various directions, and it is one of the fundamental errors of our time – if I may digress once more – that theology is all too often mistaken for religion itself. The explanation of how the piece works is no substitute for the music.

You can see this development in today's worship services, where the sermon has over time taken on greater and greater importance – especially in Christianity since the Reformation of the sixteenth century, and later in Judaism and Islam as well. And why? I suppose it's because the people were less and less willing to accept a belief unexamined. And so I don't want to criticize the priest at your school's prayer service advocating aiding refugees or warning about climate change; it's important, as I said, not just to read the holy scriptures, but to understand them from a contemporary perspective. I only want to point out that the sermon alone does not make a worship service.

In the Eastern churches, the priest's lecture even today is often insignificant, taken care of in 2, 3 minutes, in a Mass that can easily last 6, 7 or even 10 hours. The rest of the service consists of singing and melodic recitations, the precisely rehearsed choreography of the monks, and a symphony of lighting effects, bells, rattles and smells. I have seen such an Orthodox liturgy a few times myself, and although I naturally didn't understand a word, it moved me more deeply than an ordinary worship service in Germany, whether in Cologne Cathedral or in the Central Mosque – deep in my psyche, where language can't reach.

Understanding is important – I mean, understanding with your mind. But you can't understand unless you first see, hear, breathe, smell, touch, feel. In Georgia, in Kosovo, in Greece and in Armenia, I saw, heard, breathed, smelled, touched, felt the richness of a tradition that has been passed on orally from teachers to students for a thousand, two thousand years, without written records, without a curriculum. I saw, heard, breathed, smelled, touched, felt what contemplation means: not meditating for a half hour or jogging for an hour as I do, but a whole life in silence and prayer, where even mealtimes are spent listening to the Bible, the monks taking turns reading aloud. In the remote monasteries I saw, heard, breathed, smelled, touched, felt what a community is in which every penny is shared, and also the beauty of religion when every gesture harmonizes as if by magic with every smell, every change in the light with every sound. And because no one spoke to me, I also saw, heard, breathed, smelled, touched, felt inside myself.

Gradually, I grew accustomed to a time that is not measured in minutes.

Human beings consist of more than just a mind. Nature and spirit, birth and death, love and hate, illness and healing, peace and war – life is full of experiences that touch us in our soul, resonate in our psyche, throw our feelings all topsy-turvy. It makes us happy; it gives us gifts; but then life also overwhelms us again and again, leaves us perplexed and sad; it holds loss and pain. And God too is at the same time powerful and tender, terrible and compassionate, beautiful and baffling, sublime and . . . ninety-nine epithets just in Islam, and each one stands for a different colour of our own reality. His message consists not only of sentences that make sense the moment we hear them: it also consists in the fact of language itself, and often in the very places where words are as strange and mysterious as reality – in the sound, the melody, the rhythm, the metaphors, the sentences that are hard to parse, in which even a philologist can't say for certain what the subject is, the object, the verb, or whether a part of the sentence is missing altogether.

Just think: it used to be mandatory – mandatory! – for a Muslim theologian to be an expert on poetry, phonetics and singing; many of the most famous Quran scholars also wrote poetry themselves. And, even today, it goes without saying that Muslims always listen to the surahs in the original Arabic too, and recite them in Arabic in ritual prayer. In olden times, it never would have occurred to any scholar to depend solely on a translation of the Quran. So you can imagine how outraged I am by the self-proclaimed imams on YouTube – who know nothing about anything, nothing about the history of our theology, nothing about other religions, nothing about literature, nothing about the Arabic language, except to screech *Allāhu akbar* after every sentence. The Quran is not a search engine for all of today's questions, from beard styles to democracy!

I know, you're going to think I'm overgeneralizing again. And, since anyone who has a different opinion from your

father must be right, you may even go as far as to defend the
hate preachers, who have just as much right to interpret the
Quran as I have.

All right, then, let me be more specific. I warn you, though,
it's going to get a bit more complicated in the next Extra
Section. Because being specific doesn't mean simple, but more
precise. Imagine this was, let's say, a book on physics: what
comes next would then be the boring section with the equa-
tions. To be honest, in Stephen Hawking's books sometimes I
see only mumbo-jumbo, but still, when I try in vain to decipher
his letters, numbers and mathematical operators, I do get the
impression that physics is a very exact science. The philology
I studied is also an exact science inasmuch as it puts language
under a microscope.

Extra Section for Everyone Who Wants to Learn a Little Arabic!

I'd like to show you the importance of form using a tiny example, the beginning of Surah 101. To do this, I'll have to read you
not just the translation, but the Arabic original, because *qur'ān*
means, literally, 'recitation'. What was revealed to Muhammad
was not a book – not a written text at all. No, he heard a recitation in a dream, and he didn't write it down, but sang it to his
compatriots: *Rattili l-qur'āna tartila*, says Surah 73, verse 4 –
'Sing the Quran singingly!' There are countless stories of Arabs
who converted to Islam because they found the recitation so
beautiful – not edifying, not profound, not instructive, but
beautiful! And when the early Muslims wanted to introduce
the Quran to other peoples, they didn't just send them manuscripts, but, every time, they also sent a reciter who knew all
114 surahs by heart. And in case of discrepancy, what counted
was the reciter's memory, not the written document! Don't try
to imagine that in today's terms, in which books are something

very common and, since the invention of the printing press, can easily be produced in many copies. In Muhammad's time, manuscripts were little more than memory aids, or what sheet music is to an opera singer: what counted was not what the eyes could see, but what you could hear. For the Quran, that's still true today.

In the unlikely and inexplicable case that you put your hands over your ears when I begin to sing Surah 101, we can also listen to a professional recitation on YouTube, by a classic reciter such as Abdulbasit Abdulsamad, for example, or a younger one if you like, such as Abdelkarim Edghouch. If you'd rather hear a female voice, I suggest Maria Ulfah, who is a star in Indonesia, or the Canadian Seemi Bushra Ghazi.

1	*al-qāri'a*	The *qāri'a*.
2	*mā l-qāri'a*	What is the *qāri'a*?
3	*wa mā adrāka mā l-qāri'a*	And what makes you know what the *qāri'a* is?

The first verse consists of a single word: *al-qāri'a*. The first syllable *al* is the Arabic definite article, as for example in *al-jabr*, which in Latin became *algebra*; in *al-kuhl*, which we know as *alcohol*; and in many more loan words, most of which immigrated to Europe via Andalusia – even the Spanish national cheer *¡Olé!* contains an *al*: from *al-lāh*, 'the God'.

And *qāri'a*? Well, the word *qari'a* is practically unknown, and not only to us, but also, as the surah implies, to the Arabs of Muhammad's day.

In the structure of the Semitic languages, which include Arabic and Hebrew, three consonants are ordinarily enough to identify a field of meanings in which many different words can be derived by certain rules (as we have seen in the case of *s–l–m* and words that have to do broadly with peace: *salām* and *shalom*, *islām*, *muslim* and so on). In the case of *qari'a*, the three consonants are *qāf*, *rā* and *'ayn*, the last of which is a voiced pharyngeal consonant that has no counterpart in the Latin alphabet. Together, they identify a field of meanings that ranges from 'strike' to 'shock', and also to 'pound' and 'break'. Hardly any other Arabic text contains the word form used here with these consonants, a feminine participle – that is, 'the person or thing striking', or 'shocking', 'pounding', 'breaking'. You might say this surah starts with a word that it invents itself. The uncertainty of the meaning is compounded by the vagueness of the sentence, since al-qari'a is completely isolated here, not joined with any verb, object or adjective; just al-qari'a, with the qāf and the 'ayn pronounced so deep in the pharynx that they make the chest vibrate.

Imagine: what would you say if someone in panic were to shout in English an unintelligible word, something about pounding, striking, breaking or something like that, in a low tone welling up from deep in their throat? You'd say, What? And Muhammad's listeners too probably said, What?

And what does the Quran do? Instead of giving an answer, the second verse expresses precisely this question: Mā l-qāri'a – 'What is the qāri'a?' In doing so, the surah draws out the suspense caused by the enigmatic first verse by withholding the answer a second time. You still don't know what the qāri'a is!

And the answer is not forthcoming in the third verse either; on the contrary: wa mā adrāka mā – 'What makes you know . . .?' – poses a new riddle. Because the solution that follows this could refer both to the initial question ('What is the qāri'a?') and to that which teaches the answer to the question ('What makes you know what the qāri'a is?'). Both are grammatically possible. That means it is purposely left up to you how you choose to understand the question. In either case, the answer given is as follows (I will continue to translate as literally as possible):

4	yawma yakūnu n-nāsu	A day when the people are
	ka-l-farāshi l-mabthūth	as scattered moths,

5 *wa takūnu l-jibālu*   and the mountains are as
   ka-l-ʿihni l-manfūsh   tousled wool.

Still no answer! Instead, another ambiguous sentence structure and two mysterious images. Even the first word, simple as it may seem – *yawma*, 'a day' – is ambiguous: it could mean 'think of a day . . .', but it could just as probably mean 'on a day . . .'.

Do you notice the difference?

If you understand *yawma* one way, as the direct object of an implied verb – 'Think of a day . . .' – then the answer that follows refers to the question 'What is the *qāriʿa*?'

If you understand *yawma* the other way, as a temporal adverb – 'On a day when . . .' – then the answer refers to the question 'What makes you know what the *qāriʿa* is?'

Pretty complicated, isn't it? Very fiddly work, this philology. And so far I've only analysed the words.

So now let's look at the two similes that we find in the fourth and fifth verses: people like scattered moths, and mountains like tousled wool.

This seems mysterious at first glance – but why, actually? The words themselves are drawn from everyday life and familiar to anyone: people, moths, scattered; mountains, wool, tousled. So the eerie effect is caused not so much by the words themselves as by their strange, unexpected combination: what are people lying around like scattered moths supposed to suggest? Or mountains looking like tousled wool? The Arabs of the seventh century may have imagined a supernatural sandstorm, or a severe thunderstorm. Today we would be more likely to think of a toxic spill or a nuclear war. One way or the other, just five short – extremely short – verses at the opening of Surah 101 create a feeling of impending doom if humanity does not change its ways.

And the form is a part of that message. The same surah in different, 'understandable' sentences would create a different, less menacing effect – try it yourself by retelling the beginning of Surah 101 in your own words!

And even if you recounted all the possible meanings contained in every single verse, you would have nothing more than that information, and you still wouldn't experience the feeling. But learning – and this should be true in school as well, in every single subject – is much more than information; learning is receiving instruction, acquiring structure: building up, giving shape to something. Learning is formative in the way an experience can be formative: that is, it can affect your shape or structure. That makes translating the Quran, or poetry for that matter, very difficult – much more difficult than the Bible, by the way, which consists mostly of stories and not so much of poems. Stories can be varied, reshaped, retold in modern language – as a child I loved the children's Bible that we read in school. But what do you do with the rhymes, rhythms and sounds that verses are made of? The hints and ambiguities, the sentence fragments, gaps and enigmas, the strange and solemn feeling evoked by the old-fashioned language itself?

End of the Extra Section for Everyone Who Wants to Learn a Little Arabic!

This brings me to one of the basic properties of poetry, which I would also like to explain using a short example. This time, let's take not the Quran, but one of Goethe's most famous, and at the same time shortest, poems: the 'Wanderer's Night Song'. Perhaps the most faithful English translation of it is that by Henry Wadsworth Longfellow:

Über allen Gipfeln	O'er all the hill-tops
Ist Ruh',	Is quiet now,
In allen Wipfeln	In all the tree-tops
Spürest du	Hearest thou

Kaum einen Hauch;	Hardly a breath;
Die Vögelein schweigen	The birds are asleep in the
im Walde.	trees:
Warte nur, balde	Wait; soon like these
Ruhest du auch.	Thou too shalt rest.

What's happening here? The poem draws a picture with just a few strokes of the pen: the view from a mountaintop of the forest and mountains round about in the twilight. And this image of the silence of nature as the world sinks into darkness suggests human mortality. But the feeling that comes over you is evoked not so much by the words, which are very simple; the feeling is created by the melody of the verses, especially by the threefold cadence from the front vowels (i, e, a) to the back vowels (o, u), which are automatically lengthened at the ends of the lines: '*all – now*', '*all – thou*', '*like these / Thou too*' – as if you yourself would soon descend from the sphere of life down into the earth, give up the ghost, and become one with nature. Outdoors, under the open sky, everyone has been gripped by such melancholy at some time – precisely where the world is tranquil, as if enchanted: in the mountains, towards evening, in the silence when the birds stop singing. Only, if I wanted to describe this atmosphere myself, when something is both beautiful and sad, both living and silent as a tomb, I would have to compose an essay. Goethe, however, manages to evoke this paradoxical feeling in a very few lines and in a simple and yet memorable sequence of sounds, from the high, bright front vowels to the low, dark back vowels.

We often think, Ah, these poets! they go on so long and loud to say what could be said in two words. And yet the opposite is the case: poetry is distilled meaning – saying much in few words. Because the text is open, it offers gaps that every reader, every listener fills out of their own lives, their own personality, their own mood. Perhaps you could explain it something like this: our normal language is like drawers or folders where we store everything we experience. And that's necessary, because otherwise we couldn't make appointments, write exams or plan bike trips. But reality is often too complex, too crazy, too mysterious for an experience to fit in a particular drawer, or in any drawer: just suppose a person is happy and sad at the same time, or their feelings of love and hate are mixed together – that happens! And for all the fluttery, fiddly, complicated things that we can't express in our day-to-day language, but that actually make up the core of reality – for that, there is poetry. Poetry is the quantum physics of language, so to speak.

I started today's chapter by telling you about the Orthodox Masses I attended in Eastern Europe. To close, let me also tell you about a Muslim ritual – a Sufi gathering, to be more precise – in Sarajevo, the capital of Bosnia, not all that far away from here. 'Sufi' is what the mystics in Islam are called. The word is derived from *sūf*, 'wool', because the mystics were once distinguishable by their simple garb of homespun wool. The Sufis cared little for outward appearances – neither for the power of kings nor for prestige or possessions. Having no needs made the Sufis free – think about that next time before you ask for a raise in your allowance.

The Sufis in Sarajevo wear ordinary clothes, but they still share their possessions with the poor. After the ritual prayer, the shared meal and the words of their pir, or 'eldest', who spoke about love, we all knelt in a circle: thirty, forty believers, old and young, men and women, rich and poor. The pir closed his eyes and murmured *Allāh*, 'God', and everyone joined in: '*al*' on inhaling, '*lāh*' on exhaling, over and over – *Al-lāh, al-lāh, al-lāh*, like sighing out loud. Our torsos spontaneously rocked back and forth like a wave, tensing backwards on '*al*', releasing forwards on '*lāh*', over and over, again and again, for maybe a half hour, maybe an hour: '*Al-lāāāh*', with this trembling in my ribcage, like with the Indian *Om*, until I slipped into a trance, a rapture of happiness. And the strange thing was, the breathing made me feel not only connected with the Creator, filled with the Creator: at the same time, I felt connected with these unknown women and men who were likewise being permeated by our breathing. When it was over, I looked warmly at the eyes all around, and the eyes all around looked tenderly back at me. That closeness, to people and to God at the same time – to the finite and the infinite both at once: there's no way you can think that; you can only experience it. It's as if you wanted to explain to someone who has never been swimming what it feels like to dive into the water.

A human being doesn't consist of just a mind. And that is true in everything you experience: happiness, love, desperation, grief, friendship; and it's the same in religion. Praying is not just an act of the rational mind, but involves the psyche, the soul, the body – when I stand to pray and spread my arms, bow, prostrate myself, kneel, stand up again and, finally, run my hands over my face from top to bottom, as if I were taking off the spell of God again to return to ordinary life.

But this here, the book your grandpa has asked me to write, happens to consist of whole sentences – subject, verb, object – and so we will have to bear with the difficulty of trying to talk about the ineffable, probably right through to the last page. And we won't get through it without poetry.

From Gods to God

Yesterday, you said the Christians had an advantage if the Bible is so much easier to translate than the Quran. That's probably true. Every religion has its advantages, and also its disadvantages. It's hard to get used to the abysmal pessimism of Buddhism, which sees only pain and suffering in life – and yet it would seem to be possible, as you can see from the many sculptures of a laughing Buddha. Day-to-day life in the modern world is not exactly easy for Orthodox Jews who obey the many rules of correct behaviour – just imagine you weren't allowed to flip so much as a light switch on Saturdays. The Christians have to grapple with original sin, and the Catholics with celibacy (that is, the rule against priests marrying). Our religion has its difficulties too, and yesterday evening you put your finger on one: on the one hand, Islam, perhaps more than any other religion, is bound to a certain language, namely Arabic; but on the other hand, Islam is addressed to all people. The German poet Friedrich Rückert, who lived in the nineteenth century, wrote a poem about this paradox:

| *Den Christenbüchern ist* | The Christian scriptures |
| *ein großer Vorzug eigen,* | have a great advantage: |

Vor dem beschämet die des	Each people can retell them
Islams müssen schweigen;	in its native language
Der Vorzug, daß sie leicht in	And in each land around the
alle Volksmundarten	world they find revival.
Zu übertragen sind auf allen	This the Islamic revelation
Weltumfahrten.	cannot rival:
Des Korans Redeschmuck	The verse of the Quran
geht rettungslos verloren,	cannot survive translation;
Der Bibel Einfalt wird	The Bible's stories are
dadurch neu geboren.	reborn to every nation.
Daher mag eher die, als	The latter therefore
jener, Segen stiften,	everyone to bliss may lead;
Gleich einem Samen, der	In any soil may grow the
gedeiht auf allen Triften.	fruit of hardier seed.

But do you know what? Difficulties often stimulate creative solutions. Rückert, for example, found that the Quran was untranslatable, all right – and what did he do then? Set about translating it himself, and quite splendidly. And the Iranians, the Turks, the Indonesians and the Senegalese have gradually found their way to an Islam of their own, which is a bit different from Arabian Islam. And among us who were born in Europe, too, an Islam will gradually take shape which will also be a little bit different, but will be right at home here. We haven't been here very long yet. Three generations: that's no time at all to a religion.

You probably aren't interested in such details, I know. Yesterday, in fact, you said you'd had quite enough of language and poetry – it's always gratifying to hear you hold my profession in such high esteem. You wanted me to finally get around to saying who God is.

Is that all? It doesn't take much to satisfy you, does it?

Who God is, who God is . . . What I can tell you instead is a story – anyone anywhere can understand a story. It's a story by Rumi, the greatest Persian poet of the thirteenth century, although he lived most of his life in what is now Turkey. As a result, the Turks call him the greatest Turkish poet of the thirteenth century. What if the different countries still fought over poets today, instead of oil or power? The battles would almost be fun! Instead, poets in Turkey get arrested nowadays, and in Iran still more.

Maybe you've heard of the whirling dervishes in Konya, or seen videos on the Internet: originally, these were the disciples of Rumi, who often composed poems while dancing, and you can still feel the dizziness, the ecstasy, in his poems, even in translation. He's become a real celebrity in America lately, and pop stars like Madonna have put his verses to music – then they sound like this: 'My heart is burning with love, yeah!' But Rumi was also a gifted storyteller who collected countless folk tales and transformed them to give them a mystical meaning.

Mystical – I always assume you know what that means. But perhaps I should . . . no, not another explanation already; for now, just listen to one of these stories.

An elephant wandered into a village where the inhabitants were blind. The people were much amazed at its great size, and they touched the big animal, each one in a different place. It must be a snake! cried one of them, whose hand ran along the elephant's trunk; a giant snake! No, it is trees, said the second, standing between the elephant's legs, trees or tree trunks. It is definitely leather, said the third, feeling the animal's belly. No, it is soft and wet, said the fourth, touching the elephant's tongue. You call that soft? asked the fifth, who had bumped against one of the tusks. It moves so quickly back and forth! said the sixth in amazement, standing by the tail. It is a throne! the seventh pronounced, sitting on the elephant's back. And so on and so forth . . . everyone in the village of the blind had a different idea of the elephant, although it was one and the same animal.

So, now, who is God? Or perhaps the question ought to be: *what* is God? Because we haven't yet established that He's a person, or for that matter a specific, clearly delimited being. It's not even generally established whether there is only one God. Many religions, if not most of them, teach that the gods are numerous, just as human beings are. In that case, religion is a relationship of many to many.

Islam, like Christianity and Judaism, is clearly distinct from other religious doctrines on this point: Islam, Christianity and Judaism have only one God. For that reason, they are called monotheistic religions, which simply means religions in which God is unique ('mono' is Greek for 'one' or 'only', and 'theism' means more or less 'the doctrine of God'). Hinduism, the religions of the Native Americans, and the pantheon of the ancient Greeks, with Zeus, Athena, Hermes and so on, are polytheistic ('poly' is also Greek and means 'many', 'multiple'). Now you also understand why the first clause of the Islamic profession of faith says so prominently, *Lā ilāha illa llāh* – there is no god except God: because the ancient Arabs were also polytheists; that is, they revered many gods. Islam adopted the Jews' and the Christians' belief that all the other gods don't exist – *lā ilāha* – there is just the One and Only: *illa llāh*. The prayer we say incorporates the short Surah 112, which I will read to you in the translation of Friedrich Rückert. Yes, that same Rückert who held the Quran to be untranslatable, and then translated more than a few verses so ingeniously:

Sag: Gott ist Einer,	Say: God is One,
Ein ewig reiner,	God the Eternal one,
Hat nicht gezeugt, und ihn	Engendered no other and
gezeugt hat keiner,	was engendered by none,
Und nicht ihm gleich ist	And like Him there is not
einer.	one.

Imagine a time when there was no technology, neither smartphones nor refrigerators, nor even rainproof clothes, nor anything synthetic at all, no concrete, no steel, and of course no bicycles, trains or cars, no electricity, no heat, and no running water. The doctor had only his herbs, the dentist only his forceps, and the surgeon – well, better not imagine how operations were carried out before anaesthetics had been invented. In those days, human beings were subjected to the forces of nature quite differently from today – helplessly almost. In the hot, dry countries, people were dependent on the rains, without which the wells would dry up and the crops would wither. In the cold countries, people starved when the winter was longer than usual, because their stored food ran out and all the seedlings froze. In the forests, people were afraid of snakes and wild animals lurking everywhere. In the mountains, there was the danger of rockslides, avalanches and sudden changes of weather.

Those the most threatened by nature, though, were wanderers: the messengers, merchants, soldiers, caravans, refugees. Anyone trying to get from here to there would be shaken to the marrow by every thunderstorm, every sandstorm, every heat wave and every cold snap. Travellers were dependent on the sun to warm them and light their way, and at the same time they dreaded the heat. They thirsted for water, and at the same time they feared the deluge. They hoped for rain even while they feared the storm. They ate animals, and at the same time they feared they might be eaten by them. And so on and so forth. It was the same nature that menaced people and protected them, provided for them and starved them, slaked their thirst or dehydrated them, kept them alive or killed them. Nature had many faces; some were horrible, others pleasant and gentle. And there wasn't just one animal, but many different kinds: some useful and loyal, others dangerous and unpredictable. Thus, over time, many gods developed that incorporated the various unfathomable natural phenomena: the god of the seas and the god of the sun; the god of the wild animals and the god of the domesticated animals – and gods that represented all the various and opposing human experiences: the god of love

and the god of hate; the god of peace and the god of war; the
god of light and the god of darkness.

But at some point in human history, people realized that,
behind all the different phenomena, impressions, and feelings,
and thus behind all the different gods, there was just one principle, a life principle so to speak.

> Among His signs are
> Day and night, sun and moon.
> Do not bow down to the sun, nor to the moon!
> Bow down to God, Who created them.
>
> Surah 41:37

People realized – saw, heard, breathed, smelled, touched, felt –
that everything, from themselves down to the ants, the plants
and even the microbes, was descended from a common origin
(as science found much later with the discovery of evolution).
And this single life principle, the common origin of all creatures and the unity of all opposites, is what, or who, we call
God.

Now this may be just a fourth and still provisional explanation, following on my attempts to explain God by reference to
infinity, then to breathing and, in the last chapter, to nature:
the first principle of all being. But we have a few chapters
ahead of us. And when the book comes to an end, you'll still
have many years of life ahead of you in which you will continue
to wonder who or what God really is. Maybe the important
thing isn't finding the answer, but that you never stop asking
the question – because the question itself is that relationship
that we have with God. A person who has the answer is done;
they don't need to search any more; they spend the time con-
gratulating themselves. But a person who asks is addressing
someone. And where God is concerned, you can ask all you
want: you'll always find new answers, depending how your life
is going, whether you're young or old, in love or sad, happy or

distressed. And there can be no end to the questions, because God is endlessness itself, and so the search for Him can never end.

Is there such a thing as One True Religion? you may be wondering at this point.

Of course, says Islam: Islam itself is the one, the true, religion. However, the Prophet also says that the ways to God are as numerous as the breaths a person takes; and he also makes it plain, over and over again, that he is no better, smarter or more enlightened than all the other prophets before him. So which is it?

Surah 14, verse 4, says:

And We have not sent a messenger
But in the language of his people,
That he speak clearly to them.
And God lets stray whom He will;
He is the Mighty, the Wise.

The message of God is basically the same, and he sends messengers – that is, prophets – to all peoples, to proclaim the message in each people's own language, to fit their time and culture. Muhammad is the messenger through whom God revealed Himself to the Arabs. If there is one thing in the Quran that distinguishes him from the other prophets, it's this: the Quran declares Muhammad the 'Seal of the Prophets'; he brought God's word in its final version, so to speak, which the Arabs then carried to other countries so that it gradually spread over half the world. But that doesn't mean the earlier revelations are no longer valid. On the contrary, other prophets too are accorded special status in the Quran: Moses is 'the Word of God'; Abraham 'the Friend of God'; Jesus 'the Spirit of God'. And Jesus is explicitly called 'Christ' in the Quran – that is, Redeemer or Messiah. You can tell that to your Religious Education teacher at school; she probably doesn't know that

Jesus is the Christ in Islam too. And how should she, when most of the Muslims themselves have forgotten it?

Your grandpa always used to say – and I can still hear the same sentence as my own grandparents used to speak it in Isfahan – anyone who calls Christians or Jews unbelievers can't be a good Muslim. And your grandma, when I was much smaller than you are now, explained it to me this way: so many paths have led to God, everywhere in the world, since the dawn of humanity, before there was Islam, and we Muslims are just lucky that our path is a little straighter and has fewer wrong turns, because it's the last one God laid out. We're on the motorway, you might say. The other paths have a few bumps and potholes here and there, and some of the signposts aren't quite accurate any more. But, of course, they also lead to God; they only take a half hour longer; you only need two, three good deeds more.

I suppose even this little advantage that we attribute to Islam offends your sense of justice. But, you know, I don't think it's a bad idea for people to think their own religion is the ideal one. If everything had the same value, as you seem to wish it did, all the religions would dissolve into one grey mass. That would be a terrible loss, not only of insights, points of view, sounds – after all, music, painting, poetry and philosophy too have their origins in each culture's own religion. To take just German culture, Bach, Beethoven and Schubert, Gryphius, Goethe and Kafka – whether they personally believed in God or not, the works they created are lavish with motifs, questions, images from the Bible, from church hymns, from the lives of the saints, from Christian and Jewish mysticism.

But the religions themselves would also lose their energy and their fascination if they were all indistinguishable from each other. All the different clothes, which cover the same truth, are not just pretty to look at and bear witness to the diversity and the splendour of the human mind – no: they are absolutely necessary, because the circumstances, the living conditions and the experience of the peoples are all different. Besides, it's a good idea to choose one path out of the many that lead to your destination. If you constantly alternate between different roads, because one has the best signposting, another the best surface and a third the best rest stops, you won't make any headway.

Perhaps we can compare it with love. After all, love is feeling someone is special, unique, a taste of heaven; whether it's your wife, your husband or your child. If you loved all people the same, you would never be in love. Is it so different with religion? People think theirs is the right one; that's just how it is; and the more certain they are, the less sense it makes to them that someone else might see God differently. This passion is the source of strength and creativity, courage and sacrifice, just as lovers develop incredible energy where their beloved is concerned. But people also realize, if they only take a step back, that their point of view is not the only one possible. And, conversely, if they step closer, as the mystics in all religions do – in contemplation, in meditation, and also in song, dance, poetry and, not least, in the love of their fellow human beings, who are also God's creatures – if they come so close that they leave their own influences, preferences, prejudices behind them, they see God in every form. Just as a leaf of our chestnut tree looks very different, and surprisingly new in each perspective, when you look at it from 10 metres away or 10 centimetres – to say nothing of looking at it under a microscope.

> To each of you We have given a law and a path;
> If God had so wished, He would have made you a single
>   community –
> But He wanted to test you in what He has given you.
> So contend in good works!
> You will all return to God,
> And He will explain what you disagreed on.
>
> Surah 5:48

The contradiction between the outward religion, which is unique, and the inner message, which recognizes other truths as well, is found not only in Islam. Although the Bible declares them the chosen people, Jews do not take that as a reason to look down on other peoples. Although the Christian Gospel unmistakably states that no one comes to the Father except through Jesus Christ, and all others will burn in Hell, including us Muslims, it is that same Gospel that teaches Christians to love not just their neighbour, but their enemy, and many Christians especially are charitable to strangers regardless of their religion. Eventually, even the church had to admit that other religions also have a share of the truth, although the Bible doesn't say so in so many words. The church had to admit it because that's what love teaches.

> See, they who believe, and the Jews, Christians, Sabaeans –
> Whoever believes in God and the Last Day and does right,
> Their reward is with their Lord,
> Fear shall not come over them,
> And they shall not sorrow.
> Surah 2:62

It never would have occurred to your grandparents, or mine, to try to persuade a Christian or a Jew to accept Islam. They would have been more likely to urge Christians or Jews to take their own faith seriously. And, to be honest, it was painful to them, especially towards the end of their lives, that the charity of many Jews and Christians seemed more devout to them than the religious zeal they saw in the Islamic world. Even your great-grandfather, who visited our family in 1963, came to the conclusion that the Europeans were actually much better Muslims. I'll read you the passage from his memoirs:

> I told my wife we would do well to think about whether this freedom within reasonable limits that we have found among

the Franks wouldn't be better than the egoistical anarchy that we know in Iran. For it is chaos, selfishness and cruelty that have driven us to ruin. To be honest, in our country everyone thinks only of himself, of his own petty self-interest, instead of the welfare of his fellows. And yet we Muslims all grew up with the divine word that a Muslim is one by whose hand and by whose word no harm comes to anyone. Now let us consider, madam, whether by this definition we are the Muslims, or the people here whom we call unbelievers, and of whom we say that they deserve Hell.

Yes, that's how people talked in those days: the Iranians sixty years ago, and a hundred years ago the Germans too. The Muslims still called the Europeans Franks, and to the Europeans the Muslims were still Mohammedans. Married couples addressed each other as madam and mister, and I myself, as you know, have never once used the familiar form in addressing my parents, as children today naturally do, not just in Germany, but in Iran too. I can't decide which is better, the closeness of today or the respect of those days – I only want to say that, along with the language, relations between people naturally change everywhere, even such personal relationships as a marriage, or those between parents and children. And our relationship to God naturally changes in this way too, all over the world. If the faithful in olden times had too much respect, too much dread and servility, today the opposite is the case: they speak to God perhaps all too much as equals, as if God was their pal who lives next door.

But that's not what we were talking about . . .

. . . where was I?

Ah, I remember: on his visit to Europe, your great-grandfather found societies that seemed to him more just, more free, more tolerant than his own. Iran was ruled in those days by a brutal dictator, the Shah, and although the people carried out a revolution in 1979, the arrests and killings of people who take to the streets to demand free elections have long since begun again. Do you know what your great-grandpa did on his travels in Europe when it was time for his prayers? He went to the nearest church and unrolled his little prayer rug beside the pews. And, in 1963, no pastor had any objection. What a long time ago that was. And what a good thing Great-grandpa didn't visit Europe 20 years earlier: in 1943, he wouldn't have gained such a favourable impression of the Franks. And 20 years from now, you will have a more hopeful view of Iran, whose courageous and loving people will certainly win their freedom.

When I was a child, discussions like this – who is a believer and who's not – were not theoretical to me. Just like you, I was born a Muslim in a country where the vast majority of people belong to a different religion, or to none at all. None of my friends were Muslims, and in spite of that – in spite of it? – of course I liked them a lot. Imagine if my parents had said to me back then, Robbie and Johnny are lovely boys, but in spite of that – in spite of it? – they're going to burn in Hell because they happen to be unbelievers. I would sooner have turned apostate myself, I think, than accept that my friends were in peril of damnation. Fortunately, I heard Grandpa say over and over again:

> Whoso greets you wishing you peace,
> Do not say to them: You are not a believer.
>
> *Surah* 4:94

And besides – your grandma said, a few years ago when I mentioned her explanation about the different paths – besides, our path, Islam, is overgrown with a great deal of moss by now, strewn with gravel and even big, sharp boulders on which it's all too easy to hurt yourself. Since then, I think, every time I hear on the news about a terrorist attack that the Islamists have committed, or when I see a little girl in our neighbourhood, 4 or 5 years old, whose parents make her wear a headscarf – I think, yes, Islam is sorely in need of road maintenance.

To God Belongs the Orient, to God Belongs the Occident

O h God, motorways are totally stupid, you say – people should take the train. Okay, it was a bad analogy – but it was your grandma's, not mine! And, 50 years ago, even you would have thought motorways were brilliant; no one was talking about climate change or the environment back then. When I was a child, for example, I wanted to be a Formula 1 driver, and that was normal in those days. That's why I asked your grandma why Islam is just a slow-moving motorway and not a racetrack. And now you want Islam to be a railway platform, or maybe a cycle lane?

Your other objection strikes me as more serious: it's not right, you said yesterday, the way I talk about all the people who believe in not just one God, but many gods; you said I mustn't put down polytheism as nothing but a precursor of monotheism, as if all the others – the Hindus, the Native Americans, the Native Australians, the Chinese, the non-industrial societies – simply hadn't caught on yet. We Muslims also touch only a part of the elephant, not the whole animal.

Hm, maybe you're right.

To explain what defines it, each religion has to emphasize what's unique about it – there's no getting around that; we as human beings likewise only learn our own character by contrasting ourselves with others; if we were all alone on Earth, we wouldn't know who we are. From their beginnings, Judaism, Christianity and Islam emphasized the distinction between monotheism and polytheism to set themselves apart from the earlier religions, as if believing in one God and believing in many gods were absolutely incompatible. But if God is in all things, then He is as multifarious as the world itself, and whether we call God's manifestations God or 'merely' divine may not be such a huge distinction to an impartial observer. I mean, to an atheist, we're just as crazy either way.

And yet I can't refrain from mentioning that the Quran is unequivocal on this point, and rather blunt:

> Indeed, God does not forgive placing others beside Him.
> Everything else He forgives whom He will.
> But whoever places others beside God
> Has conceived a mighty sin.
> ### Surah 4:48

Yes, polytheism is the worst sin in Islam, the only one that God does not forgive. The polytheists can therefore expect God's punishment the moment they die – the moment they die, not before! That's important, because some Muslims presume to execute God's judgement on earth. Yet the Quran says over and over that judgement is God's prerogative:

> And if your Lord had willed it,
> Everyone on Earth would have believed together.
> Will you then coerce the people
> To become believers?
> ### Surah 10:99

Those who don't know any better because no prophet has ever spoken to them are excused. But the Meccans who persisted in polytheism even though they heard the word of God were declared unbelievers and, when they continued to harass the Muslims, the Muslims fought them. Later, the Arabs conquered the surrounding countries, and while Jews and Christians were allowed to practise their religions under Islamic government, the so-called heathens were often left no other choice but to convert to Islam or be subjected, if not killed. Many rulers haven't heard even today of the tolerance expressed in Surah 109:

> Say: 'O ye unbelievers!
> I worship not what you worship,
> Nor do you worship what I worship;
> And I do not worship what you have worshipped,
> Nor do you worship what I worship.
> To you your religion and to me mine!'

The territories into which Islam expanded had been monotheistic long before Islam, so the problem of how Muslims should behave towards polytheists didn't come up that often. Only when Islam spread in India did it meet with a religion – Hinduism – in which there are undeniably a great number of gods. And what happened? Hinduism was simply declared monotheistic.

There were certainly pragmatic reasons for doing so, because the Hindus were very numerous in India and the Muslims, in the beginning, very few: they could hardly afford to make enemies of everyone else; they would have been kicked right back out. But I don't think that was the only reason. Among the Muslims who migrated to India were many Sufis, whose faith had less to do with outward forms than with seeking God in their own hearts. They were not just familiar with the Quran; they knew every single verse by heart, including Surah 2, verse 115:

> To God belongs the Orient, to God belongs the Occident.
> Whichever way you turn, you find the face of God.

The Sufis swarmed out in all directions, westward as far as Portugal, to the south as far as Africa, to the north as far as what is now Russia, eastwards beyond India to China; and everywhere they met people who took their faith just as seriously: people who prayed, who were humble, who respected every creature – remember the sadhus, the Indian holy men who walked with a broom before them so they wouldn't step on an ant. It would have gone against all reason, and still more against the insight of their hearts, against compassion, to brand all these people heretics. And suddenly Surah 17, verse 110, which had seemed at home to refer quite obviously to Islam, sounded different in their ears:

> Say: 'Call on God, or call on the Merciful;
> Whatever you call Him,
> His are the most beautiful names.'

Up to then, they had believed that this meant only their own Islamic names for God, but now the Sufis understood that all the other gods too are only different names of the same God. Maybe in India they had heard the words of Krishna, the most important of the Hindu gods: 'No matter what name you call me by, it is always I who answer.' And they responded, like the mystic Al-Jili, that the one God was revealed in the 'images of gods and the spheres and the natures and in everything that the followers of every religion and faith revere'. Those gods, Al-Jili taught, were none other than God Himself.

This was going far beyond the tolerance that the mystics found in the Quran, because tolerate, literally, means 'to endure'. This was agreement on both sides that each other's faith had its own justification. Consequently, it was not long before Muslims and Hindus prayed in the same temples, each with their own words, and in some places in India, Pakistan and Bangladesh they still do today, especially in the countryside, where mysticism has remained the customary form of religion. Great-grandpa's prayer rug in the church would have been perfectly normal in Hindustan.

There is a funny anecdote from the colonial period – the time when the British ruled India: in 1911, the colonial government wanted to find out how the Indian population was divided among the various religions. To do so, they distributed a form on which everyone could tick a box beside their religion. But many Indians had no idea whether they were 'Hindus' or 'Mohammedans', so they didn't tick any of the boxes. Two hundred thousand Indians were especially clever and wrote in their own religion below the list of options: 'Hindu-Mohammedan'. The British officials were baffled.

True, there were wars and massacres in southern Asia too, and although what was at stake was power – as everywhere – rather than religious issues, Muslims, Hindus, Buddhists, Jainists, Sikhs, Christians fought again and again in the name of their religion – with so many languages, cultures, peoples and denominations, it would have been a miracle, and historically quite exceptional, if there hadn't been such conflicts. But, overall, peace between religions was far more stable in that part of the world, which we often look down upon because of its poverty, its customs or its alleged superstitions – and often more cordial than in Europe. Sadly, common prayers are fading to a memory in many places in Hindustan, or the memory is fading to oblivion.

At this point, a Muslim theologian – and probably your Catholic Religious Education teacher too – would shout sternly: No, the believers addressed in Surah 17 verse 110 are certainly not Hindus, and by no means Chinese, Native Americans, Australians or indigenous peoples! But remember that the Sufis didn't read the Quran the way you read a law book; they sang it the way people sing poetry, and in poetry every line means something different – the meaning changes – when you hear it at home or far away in a foreign country. And here in Europe, we as Muslims are in a way in a foreign country – at least, we are few and the others are many; and the Quran wouldn't be God's word if it told us the same thing as in Iran or in a different, earlier time. If you were to ask me what the Quran teaches us Muslims of today in Europe for our day-to-day lives, I would answer first with the same saying of the Prophet that you have already heard often enough, and that I heard from my parents, and they from theirs: it is more important to be a good person than a good Muslim. And from that I would infer that it doesn't matter so much whether you, later, as a woman, wear a headscarf; whether I buy our meat from the Islamic butcher; or whether we go to the mosque on Fridays. What matters is what we have in our hearts and do for our fellow human beings, no matter what faith they belong to.

> Piety does not consist in
> Turning your faces to the East or West.
> Pious are rather they who believe in God,
> In the Last Day, the angels, the Book and the prophets,
> And who spend their money, even if they love it,
> For their relatives, the orphans and the poor,
> For the strangers, the beggars, and to redeem the slaves,
> And who perform their prayers and give alms,
> And who keep the promises they have made,
> And who are patient in misfortune, in need, or in war –
> They are the ones who are true;
> It is they who are God-fearing.
> #### Surah 2:177

Of course, there is something absolute about every religion; after all, each claims to have the truth. But God's truths are not like human truths. They transcend our logic – like nature, in which both the theory of relativity and quantum mechanics are valid – and they shimmer in many colours, like the peoples, and people, themselves. If there are different religions, it is because the peoples, and people, are different, and God speaks to every single person in the language that he or she understands. And by language I don't mean just words; I mean perceptions, images, sounds, forms, figures, other people, ideas. I would even go as far as to say that God goes on speaking after the Quran, every day, everywhere – in nature, of course, but also in us human beings if we look inward. And that is by no means just my personal opinion; for a long time, it was what the vast majority of Muslims believed, and it is written – if you read carefully – in the Quran.

'The Quran is new every time to each person who recites it', said Ibn Arabi, the 'Greatest Master' (*al-shaykh al-akbar*) of Islamic mysticism, at whose tomb in Damascus thousands of Muslims still pray today, day in and day out, even in wartime. Ibn Arabi was born in Andalusia in the thirteenth century, travelled through half the world, encountered believers of all kinds of religions, and wrote, 'God knows all the meanings of the Quran, and there is none which is not exactly what He wants to say to exactly this particular person who is listening to the Quran.'

Of course, that doesn't mean everyone can interpret the Quran however they want. Just like scientists, believers need precision, curiosity and patience to attain knowledge. They have to pay attention to the exact words, cleanse their hearts of egoism, and contemplate the sound. But when they do, Ibn Arabi writes, God holds His silent, intimate conversation with the listener, saying:

The believer learns from Me directly, but not through their reason and not through their understanding. Paradise, Hell, whether their deeds were good or bad, the Last Judgement – all that no longer concerns them; neither this world nor the next, because they stop cogitating and are all ear for what I say to them. In that moment the listener becomes the witness who sits beside Me, and it is I Myself who instruct them.

God may not have sent any more prophets after Muhammad. Nonetheless, He continues to address every single one of us in the Quran when it is recited, and in Creation, if we are attentive to nature, every moment anew; at the birth of our children, at the death of our parents, and no doubt at our own death too; in tenderness and love; to Sufis in music, in poetry and, of course, in all the other scriptures that have been revealed by God. And wherever you give to the poor, shelter a stranger, or care for an orphan, God is there. 'God taught Adam all of His names without exception, so that the Creator might be praised with every name that befits Him in Creation', Ibn Arabi teaches; 'No name is unimportant, not even the name of a big or a small spittoon.' Even a spittoon – that's a kind of jar that people used to put their saliva and their snot in long ago, before there were drains; that is, the most ordinary, base and dirty object on earth – even a spittoon, whether big or little, is to be respected, appreciated and beautifully shaped, for it too is a manifestation of God. Look around the room, look out of the window, look up in the sky, and into your own heart: to the believer, the whole world is filled with God. How could He then have disappeared from the temples of the other religions?

> And each has a direction towards which they turn;
> So contend in good works.
> Wherever you are, God will bring you together;
> Indeed, all things are in God's power.
>
> Surah 2:148

The scribes – that is, the theologians or the mullahs – don't accept such arguments as a rule, and cite other verses in which belief and disbelief are as different as day and night. Like the British colonial officials in 1911, they say, it's one or the other – tick a box. But the Islam I grew up with, the Islam in which your grandparents were brought up in Isfahan, the Islam of our ancestors and teachers is a religion of reason, of

pragmatism – that is, a religion of practical viability and, most
of all, kindness. It follows the Quran, not blindly, but asking
at every verse: what does reason say to this? What does the
heart say? And what does the Quran as a whole say to this if
we take all its apparently contradictory statements together?
This is an Islam that was predominant over many centuries,
that shaped Islamic culture more deeply than the Islam of the
scribes, and that millions and millions of Muslims carry in
their hearts today, although they may no longer be the majority. It is the Islam of our most famous poets, the Islam of Rumi,
to whom God appeared in the dance; the Islam of Hafiz, who
taught the Quran and at the same time praised pleasure, love
and, even though it is forbidden, wine. It is also the Islam of
Scheherazade, the most courageous, smartest and most imagi-
native heroine in world literature, who quotes at least a word,
a phrase or a verse of the Quran in every one of the *Thousand
and One Nights*. It is the Islam of Ibn Arabi, who wrote:

> My heart has become capable of every form:
> it is a pasture for gazelles
> and a convent for Christian monks,
> and a temple for idols
> and the pilgrim's Ka'ba
> and the tables of the Tora
> and the book of the Koran.
>
> I follow the religion of Love;
> whatever way Love's camels take,
> that is my religion and my faith.

That's all very well, but – maybe you'll object – but it's a fact that
Muhammad also waged wars. I realize you can't accept that as
a model to be emulated. And you don't have to: Muhammad is
not a god to us, and accordingly our religion isn't named after
him. We aren't Mohammedans, as the Europeans still called us

not very long ago. The position of Jesus in Christianity is quite different: to the Christians, Jesus is God, and hence perfect. Muhammad on the other hand made it clear over and over again that he was fallible; and if he was fallible, then we can criticize him. At the same time, you can't judge a person of the seventh century by 21st-century standards: that wouldn't be fair; and you would have to reject all the great minds from Plato to Augustine to Kant because they didn't have the concept of human rights that we have. They were children of their time! You have to consider the Prophet, just like all of his predecessors, and every person for that matter, in his own surroundings before you draw your conclusions. Even my progressive, absolutely reasonable views, which you at least, my child, will kindly treat as in-fal-li-ble, will be considered quite backward a hundred years from now if people then judge everything by the standards of their own time. Even your papa will be ancient history.

I know you're going to shout now: Papa, you already are!

Good gracious, yes – not that your views are going to last any longer than mine. That's why there are revelations and traditions, after all: so that at least a few ideals or principles may last longer than an individual mind.

I myself, with my admittedly limited mind, tied to its time and place, have read as much as I could and am convinced that Muhammad is one of the outstanding figures in the history of the world: a thoughtful, friendly person who was deeply inspired by God, and at the same time a loving husband, a leader who re-examined and struggled with himself again and again, a protector of orphans, perhaps because he himself had grown up without parents – and, incidentally, the greatest cat-lover among the Arabs. But, most of all, Muhammad was a revolutionary who proclaimed universal equality at a time when no one anywhere was advocating such ideas; a prophet who allowed others their beliefs; a fighter for the poor and the disenfranchised; and, yes, also a brave warrior, after he had suffered the insults, threats and attacks of the rich Meccans for many years without fighting back. And, supposing the Quran was not sent down by God, as of course all non-Muslims believe: the Quran in Arabic sounds so magical that Muhammad must, in that case, have been a great poet at least.

In Europe, and possibly in your Catholic Religious Education class, you will hear other appraisals of Muhammad – negative ones, and worse: after all, Islam was considered an enemy for many centuries, and still is by some today. I don't care to repeat the various arguments that have been fielded for and against the Prophet; there are enough books on them. Read them and judge for yourself. Least of all do I want to list the criticisms that could be raised against other religions. You can find all that for yourself, and find it persuasive or not. Every single founder of a religion had his or her qualities, strengths, severities, and if in the end you feel particularly drawn to Jesus because he was the prophet of love, then you're in the company of many Muslims, especially the Sufis. They followed Jesus, or had a particularly close relationship to him, even though they continued to revere Muhammad as the last prophet. The book that your grandpa wished is not a competition in which Islam is supposed to end up winning first place. There are enough books of that sort already, and the winner always happens to be the author's own religion.

The Tail Wags

The fact that you ask so many questions makes me glad, in theory – although practically it's keeping me from getting on with my book, which is supposed to be about God, not the history of Islam or contemporary politics.

Very well, then, taking them one by one:

First, you asked about the verses in which the Quran seems to advocate violence.

I said yesterday that, in the early years of his preaching, the Prophet patiently bore the Meccan tribal leaders' insults and attacks. Consequently, you can find many Quran verses from this period that explicitly prohibit violence – addressed to Muhammad's followers, for example, who didn't understand why they mustn't defend themselves. Later, fighting did break out, and you can find verses from this second period which seem to contradict the earlier ones because they call for resistance, including military force. However, Islamic theology has always considered these 'verses of violence' in relation specifically to Muhammad's conflict with the Meccan leaders, and not as a general injunction to kill non-believers. The purpose of theology is precisely that: to understand God's general, timeless message, which results in different statements in different

situations. Those who take these verses out of their historical context – to justify blowing up innocent people today,
for example, as the jihadists do – are not just committing an
inhuman act – no, they are also, in my opinion and in the
judgement of all reputable Muslim scholars, falsifying the message of the Quran.

Second, you asked how you should answer your Religious
Education teacher when she explains that the Quran was dis-
seminated by the sword.

You could point out to her that Western historians today
discuss back and forth why the Arabs conquered half the
world within a few decades in the late seventh and early eighth
centuries. While some cite mainly military reasons, others see
political and social causes of Islam's rapid spread. But it is
undisputed that there was great discontent with the existing
rulers when the Arabs came along. The Egyptian Christians,
for example, initially allied with the Muslims to free themselves from their Byzantine rulers, who were also Christians.
The picture is not black-and-white.

But, at bottom, your teacher is right, of course: Christians
are not the only ones who have waged wars in the name of
their religion; Muslims too conquered large parts of Asia
and Africa by force. And yet the majority of the people in
the Islamic Empire remained non-Muslim for many centuries.
The conquerors were apparently less interested in proselytiz-
ing than in expanding their dominions. Furthermore, because
non-Muslims had to pay higher taxes, the caliphs and emirs
sometimes even issued prohibitions against converting to
Islam. Not until the modern era – that is, 300, 400 years ago –
did something like a missionary movement form in Islam, and
then the Quran began to be translated into other languages.
That doesn't make Islam better or worse, more peaceful or
more violent, but it does distinguish it from Christianity,
whose mission was initiated by Jesus himself and was seriously
pursued from the very beginning.

You probably think it's stupid to want to convert other people at all – but ask your Religious Education teacher sometime whether she isn't glad that Charlemagne forced the Germanic peoples to convert to Christianity. I suspect she'll reject Charlemagne's methods and yet be grateful for her religion, which does away with human sacrifice. Similarly, I am a Muslim even though I know that the Arabs were not carrying flowers when they rode into Iran 1,400 years ago, but swords. History, which is made by human beings, doesn't erase the message that comes from God. And if you think humanity would be more peace-loving without God, then you must not have come to the twentieth century yet in your history lessons.

Third, you asked why the Baha'is, the followers of Baha'ullah, who declared himself a prophet in the nineteenth century, are persecuted in Iran.

I wish I could answer that this has nothing to do with Islam. But I'm afraid that's not true. Although Islam recognizes the earlier prophets, it has a problem with the religions that have arisen after it. Simply by existing, they contradict the assertion that Muhammad is the 'Seal of the Prophets'. And so, in the religious dictatorship that Iran became after the revolution, Baha'is are arrested, their houses and prayer rooms are confiscated, and they are forced to abjure their faith if they want to go to university or work in public administration. And yet the word for 'seal' in the Quran, *khātam*, literally means confirmation, reaffirmation or authentication of what was said before – like certifying a document by affixing a seal. It doesn't necessarily imply that Muhammad was the last prophet. But even if you reject a religion, you can still respect its followers, just as the vast majority of Christians in Germany respect us. 'A person is either a brother in faith or a brother in humanity', said Imam Ali fourteen centuries ago.

Fourth, you asked, not yesterday but the day before, whether refugees today aren't just as much at the mercy of wind and weather as 2,000 years ago.

The answer I owe you is, sadly, very short: yes, they are.

And, fifth, yesterday you asked: if everything on earth and in heaven points to God, if all the myriad phenomena are only different names of God, even a spittoon – then is the atomic bomb one, too?

That is a very good question, so good that, like all good questions, you can only answer it for yourself.

But now, back to God, Whom I do not want to blame for what human beings are responsible for.

God changes nothing about a people
As long as the people do not change what is in themselves.
Surah 13:11

So some believe in gods, others in God: objectively, I admit, that's quite a big difference. The strange thing is, though, that the greatest disagreement has not been between monotheists and polytheists. The biggest dispute arises, and almost always has arisen, where religions – like peoples, cultures, and perhaps individuals too – are the most similar. Then they fight hard for every tenth of a per cent!

But let's go ahead and look at the most important difference between Christianity and Islam:

Behold, Christ Jesus, son of Mary, is a messenger of God
And His Word which He laid in Mary
And is Spirit of Him.
So believe in God and His messengers,
And say not 'Three!'
Stop! It is better for you!
For God is a single God, praised be He –
As if He could have a son!
What is in Heaven and Earth is His.
Surah 4:171

It couldn't be said more explicitly that Jesus is not God's son. In the same verse, however, Jesus is also called 'Christ' – that is, messiah or redeemer – and he is called God's word and God's spirit. Moreover, Surah 3, verse 9, attributes to Jesus the ability, unique among all beings on Earth, to wake the dead and to make living birds out of clay – doesn't that situate him somewhere between God and humans after all? For 1,400 years, the Muslim scholars have worked hard to answer this question in the negative by emphasizing, amplifying, cementing, engraving in stone the distinction between 'Son of God' and 'Spirit of God'. After all, their whole *raison d'être* depended on their religion being unlike that of the Christians – and vice versa.

But that sounds too negative. In difference lies the richness of the world. The endeavour to be different from others gives rise to culture: distinctive songs, distinctive traditions, different religions, different foods, a distinctive literature – everything that sets an identity apart. 'Setting apart' may sound ugly, but separations are only stupid if you can't pass through them. Because, as cultures set themselves apart, they also absorb from other cultures at the same time: it takes two or more to make a dialogue; even touching – the most delicate, friendly, intimate gesture of all – implies a distance to be bridged. Boundaries – by which I mean not only geographical or political borders, but the difference and, you might say, the foreignness of people, cultures, customs – boundaries indicate that things work differently here from how they do there, which is a good thing, actually. Imagine if all people were the same, or, worse still, if all people were like us: like us Muslims, us Germans, us Iranians, us inhabitants of Cologne, us . . . – how much poorer would the world be without all the others? And even among us Muslims, Germans, Iranians, Colonians, I find it rather pleasant to be different from the others.

> And among His signs are
> The creation of the Heavens and the Earth

And the variety of your languages and your colours.
Behold, therein are signs for the knowledgeable.

Surah 30:22

Even parents, annoying as they are, have their place and their justification, if only to motivate their children not to grow up like them. But, for all their wonderful, enriching differences, Jews, Christians and Muslims forget how much they have in common. The dispute is always over the few tenths of a per cent of difference, and the less difference there is, the more seriously people take it.

I once attended a conference at which Buddhologists, Sinologists, Indologists, ethnologists, ancient-Americanists, Africanists – experts on all the different religions in the world – joined with Christian theologians, scholars of Judaism and scholars of Islam to think about what, specifically, is meant by God. And the funny thing was that the Buddhologists, Sinologists, Indologists, ethnologists, ancient-Americanists, Africanists took it for granted that we Bible and Quran scholars all belonged to one religion – everything we had to say was so similar: the same God the Creator; the same prophets; the same eastern Mediterranean origin; the three closely related languages Hebrew, Aramaic and Arabic; similar prayers; almost word for word the same commandments. And it's true: the Quran adopts so many motifs, stories, doctrines from the Bible that Islam is one of the biblical religions. That's why you would find almost everything I've been telling you, evening after evening – from the signs of God in nature to the ambiguity of scripture and the tension between the scribes and the mystics, to the worldly piety that underlies all forms of faith – in one form or another in Judaism and Christianity. But that's not all: even the clocks run differently in the three biblical religions from the rest of the world's.

The clocks?

Well, I don't mean clocks in the mechanical sense; I mean

time: the concept that time flows like a river from here to there, and history, along with all Creation, has a beginning and an end – I would have thought that was obvious. But, in fact, there is another way to experience time: namely, as a cycle in which everything comes around again, so that, ultimately, everything stays as it has always been. That kind of time can have a beginning, but it's just a first turn around the circle. To some civilizations, however, such as that of ancient China, there is no beginning; the cosmos has always existed. The important thing is that humanity, in spite of all the outward changes, has experienced basically the same thing over again in cycles, which you might compare with the seasons.

This cyclical thinking, as it was called at the conference, is found wherever there is not a single God Who created and gradually shaped the world from nothing. Without God the Creator, history doesn't exist in the form in which you learn it in school – that is, as a continuous narrative in which everything evolves in a straight line that leads to us. That means that even your history lessons, and our whole conception of the world, including our political persuasions, are derived from religion – or, to be more precise, from the belief in one God Who, in the beginning, created the universe.

Note those two terms, because you'll hear them a lot today: *cyclical* and *linear* time. In one, everything comes around again; in the other, everything builds on what went before.

As far as we know, the first monotheist was the Egyptian pharaoh Akhenaten, over 3,000 years ago. And he was the first to teach that the history of the world is a one-time process. This linear concept was passed on to Judaism via the Persian prophet Zarathustra, and persisted in Christianity and later in Islam: the world begins with the first word of God, and also ends

When the sun shall be darkened,
when the stars shall be thrown down,

when the mountains shall be set moving,
when the pregnant camels shall be neglected,
when the savage beasts shall be mustered,
when the seas shall be set boiling,
when the souls shall be coupled,
when the buried infant shall be asked for what sin she was slain,
when the scrolls shall be unrolled,
when heaven shall be stripped off,
when Hell shall be set blazing,
when Paradise shall be brought nigh,
then shall a soul know what it has produced.

Surah 81:1ff.

The complete displacement of cyclical thinking by the linear concept of time all around the Mediterranean Sea within two, three centuries, simultaneously with the rise of Christianity, is one of the most momentous revolutions in the history of the human mind. Of course, the Greek and Roman civilizations, just like ancient China and ancient India, also had histories to be written and researched. But the purpose of their history-writing was rather to find what was eternally true and always the same in spite of constant change. Thus cyclical thinking was always oriented towards the past. The history written based on linear time, on the other hand, is a study of the past in order to prepare for the future.

That sounds reasonable, and yet I could also phrase the same thing negatively: while civilizations with a cyclical concept of history continually evoke the Origin in their traditions, rituals and legends, linear thinking is oriented towards the end, or death, which it aims to overcome. I have often wondered, for example, why there are so many death scenes in our biblical religions and in our literature, while in India, Africa, China, many more stories revolve around birth. Perhaps this also has to do with the change of perspective that accompanied the belief in just one God.

In any case, a completely new conception of history spread with monotheism: the idea of progress, which has defined our modern world (and is now problematic in view of the destruction of our environment), would not have been possible without the God of the Bible and the Quran, Who created the world and will redeem it. For in Buddhism or Hinduism, salvation has a different meaning: that you as an individual escape the eternal cycle, while the world itself is bad and is not going to change. The Chinese teachings – I mean Taoism and Confucianism – have a more optimistic view of existence: for them, the cosmos has always been in equilibrium between two polarizing powers, yin and yang. So the highest challenge for human beings is to preserve or to restore this original harmony.

All this is admittedly highly simplified – my slapdash history of the religions in three, four paragraphs. But at least now I hope you understand better why, as we sat there among all the different religions, the scholars of Judaism, Christianity and Islam formed a group: not only because of our concepts, prophets and books, which all looked pretty similar, but also because of our way of looking at the world – even those individuals among us who no longer believe at all. Communism, idealism, colonialism, fascism, capitalism, existentialism – to name a few of the most important modern philosophical systems – all of them do without God, and nonetheless they can be traced back to the biblical notion that the world needs salvation. Even you kids in Fridays for Future are carrying an invisible Bible in your rucksack as you try to save the climate.

And maybe that goes to show you that religion is not some secondary topic that ought to be subsumed under Ethics in school, or dropped from the curriculum completely. No, religion is at least as important as science, history or language to anyone who wants to understand the world, whether they personally believe or not. That's why what worries me today is not so much atheism: people denying God. Atheism has always spurred religion on and obliged it to explain better. And, besides, you can't have belief at all without the freedom not to believe. No, what worries me is the spread of religious ignorance. Because, just as belief can only come about in freedom, freedom in turn depends on knowledge. If you don't know anything about religion, you're not free to reject it. In this way, freedom is not a gift, but a responsibility: it is up to you to learn to look beyond the limited horizon of your own world.

Yes, for better or for worse, our linear conception of time has spread, through the vehicle of the modern ideologies, to all continents, so that even China is governed by a Communist Party that coercively yokes the country to progress. But, as far as the religions themselves are concerned, Judaism, Christianity and Islam are still very peculiar today to believers of other faiths. Even churches and mosques don't look very different to Japanese eyes; at least, both of them have towers. And, if you remember the churches in Isfahan, and in the Orient generally, where Christianity began, the domes are the same too.

Not that the churches were originally modelled after the mosques – no, in fact it was the other way around: the Muslims adopted the round shape of the Eastern, pre-Islamic churches. But because their houses of worship were so similar, the Muslims needed a clear sign, visible from a long way off, so that the mosques wouldn't be mistaken for churches and Islam confused with Christianity. So they replaced the tower with a minaret. Later, the Christians wanted to distinguish themselves from these mosques that were being built everywhere, so they introduced a rectangular plan and pointed roofs. And so on and so forth: those who want to be distinct modify what is familiar from their neighbours. But even in doing so, they are copying it. If you want to know what churches looked like earlier, before there was Islam, you'd do better to look at the Central Mosque than Cologne Cathedral.

That doesn't mean that Judaism, Christianity, Islam are all exactly the same in the eyes of the Buddhologists, Sinologists, Indologists, ethnologists, ancient-Americanists, Africanists.

It just means there is an immediate connection between the three biblical religions. And each older religion says about each younger one – that is, Judaism says of Christianity, and Christianity says of Islam: what's new about it is false, and what's true about it is not new. Conversely, Islam says of Christianity, and Christianity of Judaism: it's a good start, but not quite perfect.

Now I suppose you want to know which of them is right.

To avoid offending your sense of justice again, let me try putting it this way: just as Christianity is an answer to questions raised by Judaism, Islam is an answer to Christianity. If you don't know the questions, you won't understand the answers. And the answers in turn raise new questions. Which means that even Islam doesn't settle everything. 'Seek after knowledge, in China if need be', the Prophet urged. Perhaps he meant that we ought to expand our view of the world there too. Because just as mystical Islam was enriched by the encounter with the Asian religions, the cyclical and linear conceptions of time can also learn from each other. It is hardly possible today, in any case, to advocate such a radical faith in progress as that which arose in the early period of industrialization. At the same time, though, I would like to stand by the idea that the world can change.

But to return again to the religious studies conference: there were greater differences just within Buddhism, with its many currents and sub-currents, than between Judaism, Christianity and Islam. To all the others – the Buddhologists, Sinologists, Hinduologists, ethnologists, ancient-Americanists, Africanists – we were just representatives of three denominations within a single biblical religion, more or less the way we talk ourselves about Sunnis and Shiites, or Protestants and Catholics. We exchanged some very puzzled looks, all right. To use Rumi's allegory of the elephant: all that Jews, Christians and Muslims argue about is whether the tail wags to the left, to the right, or around in a circle. Whether the tail must wag left after it wags to the right, or whether what seems to be wagging back and forth is actually a circular motion – that is, whether all three assertions could be true – no, you're not the first person to think of that. The mystics in Judaism, Christianity and Islam knew it long before our time. That's why they've never fought each other.

Remember the question of perspective – that is, whether we're looking at a thing from 10 metres away, or 10 centimetres, or through a microscope. Imagine you're looking down at the Earth from a hot-air balloon, or the top of a skyscraper: the people down there would all look very similar, even though every one of them is different, and loveable. That must be something like God's perspective. Except that He sees us through a microscope at the same time.

He, It – or Maybe She After All?

Yesterday evening you had only two questions.

First, doesn't the word 'perspective' presuppose a conception of God as a person, or at least as a being that has a specific location? After all, infinity can't have a perspective; it's everywhere.

Second, when are we going to have a proper lunch again and not just leftovers or sandwiches?

Okay, okay, okay.

I'm aware that my chapters keep getting longer. But that's only because I'm trying to answer your questions! If you would just believe what I tell you, then I'd have time to cook again. It works the way societies do: the ones that insist on discussing everything take a little longer. And the others are called dictatorships.

But seriously, you're right, perspective assumes that someone occupies a certain position. And only someone who is someone can create, love, redeem. So God would be something like a person after all.

That's true, by human logic, but you know my mantra by now: truths in religion go beyond what human beings are capable of thinking. Eternity, for example, doesn't just mean an extremely long time. It means timelessness. But to begin describing it, you have to use time – perhaps by remembering how you sometimes lose track of time when you're playing, or how I do when I'm listening to music; maybe that is in itself a little taste of eternity. Losing track of time means nothing less than overcoming death for a moment, however short or long.

It's the same in nature. Quantum theory, which you found so interesting, is an example of how we can measure reality to a precision of millionths of a millimetre, and still only be able to describe it in images and allegories. Imagine a quantum physicist looking through a phenomenal microscope: they don't believe anything; they just see. Or, more accurately, they measure. But what they measure is unlike everything they know on Earth, and the foundation of science: I mean things, objects, reality. And if the quantum physicists want to give a name to what they see or measure, they automatically end up with concepts: that is, things you can 'catch' or 'grasp', terms with definite outlines, simply because there's no other way they can communicate. 'Definite' means that something is delimited, bounded, and thus distinct from something else. Our thinking can't help dividing one thing from another, one second from the next, or the apple from the hand, in order to understand reality.

But what the quantum physicists recognize is not bounded; it is not matter; and hence their names for it, and ours, are not accurate. What the quantum physicists measure, and what believers feel in their beating hearts, is also a force and an act of volition for life to come into existence. I described it at the beginning of this book as endlessness; later as breath or spirit, as the ground of all being, and, most recently, as truth or true reality – but now I see that all of that sounds too passive. Endlessness, for example, can simply be still, at rest; breath is moved by a breathing being; the truth does not know itself; the ground of being is eternally unchanging. But deep inside every cell, and in the order of the whole cosmos, something concrete and intentional is at work, not just indefinite, pure being. But to be definite means to have form, properties, contours, distinctiveness. So, if God loves us, is He something like a person? The smartest answer I've heard to that question is in Hinduism. It's a paradox, of course, more or less like black light: 'God is a person and not a person.'

Now, to begin with, Hinduism has many different gods, each of them a distinct character, and at the same time it has the concept of the 'soul of the world', Brahman, which unites everything. So God is in fact a person and not a person. But also in Judaism, Christianity and Islam, where there is only one God, Who has created the world, there is no definitive answer to the question *who* God is, or whether we should think of God rather as a *what*.

The Bible and the Quran strictly forbid making images of God, only to call God in the next verse Protector, Judge, Avenger, Lover, Forgiver and so on – that is, depending how you count, ninety-nine or more all too human names. And not only that: they talk about God's throne, God's hands, God's face – what are those if not images? And these images look very much like a human being or, at least, like a person.

So I don't know whether God is a *He* or an *It*, or maybe a *She* for that matter – or all three? But I can point to what the mystics have said, the Sufis, those who have come closest to God among all Muslims. You've heard the name Ibn Arabi, and you know that he was born in Andalusia in the thirteenth century and is buried in Damascus. To many Muslims, and to growing numbers of Western scholars who study Islam, he is the most astounding and the most important person in the history of Islamic philosophy after the Prophet. It's no wonder that he has always been called 'the Greatest Master', *al-shaykh al-akbar*. Because his teachers as well as his disciples were mostly women, and he emphasized the feminine traits of God as no other mystic did, it is primarily Muslim feminists who cite him today: as early as 800 years ago, he ascribed equal rights to women, and declared them empowered to interpret the Quran, to lead Friday prayers, and to receive enlightenment from God. But we can also learn from Ibn Arabi tolerance towards other religions, emphasis on human creativity, insights into the human psyche which are nothing short of modern, and much more – and that is exactly why his books are banned today in fundamentalist countries such as Saudi Arabia, and are being rediscovered by younger Muslims all over the world.

Ibn Arabi, who acquired all the knowledge of his time, mastered the Quran by heart, including its commentaries, and left the world enough books to fill all the walls of your room – Ibn Arabi disappeared again and again to spend days, weeks, months in contemplation, meditation. And he had visions, much like those of the prophets, and his most extensive work, which fills about 2 metres of shelf space with its many volumes, is titled the *Meccan Revelations.* Meccan, because he wrote it in Mecca; Revelations, because it's based on divine inspirations and dreams.

Ibn Arabi used a great many images: sometimes God appeared to him as a beautiful woman, sometimes as a young man, sometimes as an old man, and particularly often as a mother; sometimes as a flower, sometimes as a sun, sometimes as a heavenly body; sometimes in music, sometimes in poetry and often in love – yes, in sexuality; sometimes in a Jewish man, sometimes in a Christian woman, sometimes in his own child. Whichever way he looked, there he found the face of God. And he said: What God really is must necessarily remain concealed from human beings; he would never be able to put it in words because it is beyond language, imagination, human knowledge. It is unlike everything we know; it could as well be an Everything as a Nothing. It is oneness where we humans can only think in differences – after all, the world consists, ever since the Big Bang, of difference. Even words such as love, will, energy, spirit, principle are human categories; even the word oneness, because it presupposes twoness. What is really true remains unfathomable to human beings; they can only experience God in their own words, forms, sounds, breaths. That is, they symbolize, humanize God. They call Him Father, they call Him Mother, and those who are Christians see God in a child born more than 2,000 years ago in a stable in Bethlehem. 'I am as My servant thinks Me to be', says God in a *ḥadīth qudsī*, that is, a saying transmitted by the Prophet outside of the Quran.

Do you remember the teaching of the Quran in Surah 14, verse 4, that God's message to all peoples is the same, only adapted to their times and cultures? Ibn Arabi took this idea still further: God reveals Himself not only to each people, but to every single heart in such a way as only that heart can know Him. Yes, Ibn Arabi even talks about the 'God Who is created in prayers': by that, he means that God, Who is everything and thus unbounded, takes on form only through the individual and limited human being. Yes, exactly like the air, which is always everywhere. When you breathe it in, you delimit it, shape it and mix it with your body. And if you stop inhaling air, you're dead. That is why the whole world is called in Islam 'the breath of the Merciful' – I mentioned the expression a few days ago. It originated with Ibn Arabi.

Like breath, God is in everything, and thus in every single one of us. But that also means His forms are as multifarious as His creatures. The religions point the way, but only you can find out what God is within yourself: whether as Father, Mother, Jesus or a pure principle; whether as sound, word, experience or encounter; whether in a work of art, in the study of nature, service to your fellow human beings or the conservation of the environment. But in that moment when, above and beyond all difference, you feel yourself one with all creatures in the world, because you recognize one and the same power in every other person, and even in a spittoon, then you are also one with the Creator. Ibn Arabi called this *waḥdat al-wujūd*, the 'unity of being', and that is very similar, not just verbally, to the 'singularity of consciousness', the term used by physicists

to speak of a single ordering principle connecting all experience. It is also a teaching that turns up, long before Ibn Arabi,
in the Upanishads, the earliest mystical books of India, which
are about two and a half thousand years old. In essence, it
is the core idea of every mystical tradition, including those
of Judaism, Christianity and Islam: every atom contains the
whole world; every person contains the history of all humanity;
in every soul dwells God. 'Those who know God', Ibn Arabi
writes, 'know that the relation of all beings to God is only one
relation. Therefore they witness God in everything, and nothing veils Him from them.'

Some Sufis ceased to talk about God at all. The closer they
came to Him, the less they were able to say about Him. I imagine this as if I were to move closer and closer to a big, strong
lamp – let's say, a lighthouse – until finally all the outlines of
the lamp disappear, and in the end I can only see an indefinite,
all-encompassing brightness. I wouldn't be able to see anything
for pure light, and would feel only the heat that would burn me
if I went on stepping closer and closer. God Himself says in
Surah 24, verse 35, that you can never see His light directly, but
only the reflection of it.

God is the Light of the Heavens and the Earth.
The likeness of His light is that of a niche
In which a lamp burns;
A lamp in a glass,
And the glass sparkles like a star,
Lit by a blessed tree,
An olive tree, neither eastern nor western,
Whose oil almost glows,
Although no fire has touched it –
Light upon light!
God leads to His light whom He will.
And God coins the similes for the people.
And God is knowledgeable of all things.

Other mystics prefer to say love instead of God: they believe in love, they say, and they go as far as to rephrase the *shahāda*, the Islamic profession of faith: There is no God but Love. To them, the experience of God is less a sensory impression, such as light or brightness, beauty or splendour, than a tender feeling in the heart, which they express in turn towards all creatures. And still other mystics replace the word God with the word nothing.

Does that strike you as absurd?

Yes, to our minds, it is probably absurd – that is, nonsensical: God, Who is supposed to be everything, can't at the same time be nothing. But religion is not thinking; religion is essentially experience; it is fate as lived, and as suffered, not theory. If you give it some attention, you'll notice that this experience of ours is full of paradoxes.

Just take the first and the last things we experience in life: birth and death. Living is birth and death. Could there be any greater paradox, to our consciousness, than to be born and to die? God encompasses those impressions that overtax us, and if He is everything, then He is at the same time nothing; if He is the Creator, then he is at the same time a Destroyer. Your grandpa struggled so long, four months in the hospital, back and forth between the regular ward and the intensive care unit, between hope and fear, until in the end your big strong grandpa was not only exhausted and battered – most of all, he was as helpless as a newborn baby. Nothing but peace was left in his face. Suppose someone had come to your grandpa's bedside with the definitive proof in their hands that there is nothing after death: fade to black, the end. In the spiritual state your grandpa had reached, it wouldn't have made any difference to him any more. He would have gone on being grateful and, yes, curious too. He would have wanted to know what that nothing feels like, what it is. Even nothing is something, he would have said; let's have a look. Then God would have been to him that nothing.

For the mystics too, the paradoxes resolve themselves bit by bit in this way: if not by thinking, then in their hearts. They make peace with the fact that God always includes the opposite of whatever you say He is, and life consists of birth and death, happiness and suffering, love and hate, day and night, inhaling and exhaling, constriction and release. You might also say the mystics already see death in every birth, and feel in hate the love that produces it. They are sure that death is not the end, but the opposite: a resurrection, a new birth – indeed, the real birth. To their dismay, though, the mystics are also aware, painfully aware, that peace too presupposes conflict, and by that I don't mean the two World Wars or the wars in our time in Syria, Ukraine or Yemen, which have been going on longer without the world taking much interest in them. No, humanity can well do without these wars; I will not accept the idea that so many innocent victims are necessary for some equilibrium in the world. What I mean are the wars fought in every life: a severe illness, for example, being bullied in school, heartbreak or grief; I mean each person's struggles with themselves, the doubts, the pain, the anger, the fear, the desolation. Starting with birth! God has evidently willed that life should begin with a nightmare: namely, being squeezed through a tortuous narrow passage into the unknown, towards a bright light, although the baby was probably very comfortable in its mother's belly.

The interesting thing about the verse we just looked at, Surah 24, verse 35, is not that it compares God with a light. Religions have been doing that forever. The interesting thing is the suggestion that we humans don't see the light directly – because that light is so bright it would blind us, I assume. In any case, we perceive the light of God only refracted and reflected: through the glass of a lamp, and that lamp is in a niche. The diffuse light that comes out of the niche is what we are able to recognize of God.

Once you know that, the sharp contrasts that there are between the religions dissolve, even those between polytheism and monotheism. Human beings can't help forming an idea of God; somehow they have to put this cognition, which makes up the core of all religions, into words such as 'truth', into images such as 'light', or into music, such as Schubert's sonatas that sound as if they came from another world. In such words, images, sounds, human beings have always sensed something like an order or a common origin; they feel that every being is connected with every other, and that our purpose lies in love. But these images, these words, this music – and my own clumsy explanations still more – are necessarily human. Human implies subjective, shaped by the subject's own personality, limited by the capabilities of the mind and of language. 'Inevitably, the creatures can worship only their own opinion of God', Ibn Arabi teaches; 'there are only idolaters'.

Naturally Ibn Arabi doesn't mean we are all heretics. He means that all of us, monotheists, polytheists and even atheists, the moment we peer past the boundaries of our own reality, have only the figments of our imagination. But this same imagination – that is, our creativity or capability of fantasy, which you know from playing, drawing, and especially from dreaming – is at the same time our most precious possession.

Imagination?

Yes, imagination, says Ibn Arabi: fantasy. Because the translation into language, into images, into human 'fantasies', is what makes the diffuse brightness of the divine light into something all our own, something concrete, something nameable; this translation is where the diversity is created, because human beings happen to be different: our characters, our language, our customs, the circumstances of our lives. In Greenland, people might connect that light with something warm, like the sun; in the desert, the light would be something cooling, more like the moon. Where people are still closely connected with nature, and dependent on it, they might think of animals and plants when they talk about God, or a certain mountain, which they pronounce sacred. Since more and more people have come to live in cities – that is, among other people – over the past three or four thousand years, the gods too have taken on human form. Because the men ruled in most societies, the feminine qualities of God were gradually suppressed. The more philosophical human thinking becomes, the more abstract the notions of God. 'Every being has its own God', says Ibn Arabi. He equates the universe with the totality of all the names, or qualities, that we ascribe to God: 'No individual has all of God.'

And how do you think the archangel Gabriel brought God's message to the Prophet? As a postman? Hello, package here for you? No, through the imagination, of course, which in proph- ets was much more highly developed than that of the greatest artists. That is why they only appeared every few centuries, and most often in the desert, where thoughts can wander unimpeded.

> The Messenger of God, God bless him and grant him peace,
>   said, 'Nothing will remain of the Prophet but his glad
>   tidings.'
> 'What are the glad tidings?' asked the people.
> 'The devout and righteous dreams.'
>
> Hadith

Do you know what I can't stop thinking of?

Guess.

Quantum physics? Ibn Arabi? The chestnut tree outside of our window?

No.

I can't get the word 'infinitesimal' out of my mind – the word the Russian cosmonaut used to describe the envelope of air around the earth. Do you remember? A quantity becoming 'infinitely small; approaching zero'.

The life principle, the unity of all opposites, origin, spirit, creator, eternity, infinity, omnipotence, truth, all-ordaining reality – it all sounds so big. But infinitely small? That's impossible, thinks a maths dud like me, because a thing either exists or it doesn't – but for something to get smaller and smaller, ever smaller, so that it eventually seems to border on nothingness, but without ever quite disappearing – that's beyond my understanding, and yet it's true. At least we know by now – or scientists believe they know – that the universe is continuously expanding. That is, just 20 billion years ago, the universe was smaller than a nut – no, smaller than a seed, an atom, a neutron, a wisp, a . . .

That reminds me of an anecdote about Dhu n-Nun, a famous Egyptian Sufi of the ninth century: someone challenged him, 'Show me the greatest name of God!'

Dhu n-Nun said, 'Show me the smallest!' and threw the smarty-pants out.

God is not only greater; He is also infinitesimal.

The Dark God

Yesterday's chapter was rather difficult, I admit. You found Ibn Arabi even more complicated than my philology of a few days ago. Hadn't I claimed that religion is actually something quite simple? And it is. But as soon as you talk about it, it runs through your fingers like water.

In my Arabic studies, Ibn Arabi didn't come up until near the end, and then only because I was lucky enough – or unlucky enough – to study under a professor who didn't believe in going easy on students. And here am I turning the 'Greatest Master' loose on a 12-year-old! But, you know, when I think back on university, I learned the most when I was in over my head. It didn't feel like it in the beginning – I mean, it did feel like being in over my head, but it didn't feel like I was learning. Every time the professor handed out an eleventh-century mystical treatise for us to translate by the following week, I thought at first, that's it, I'm going under. We muddled through from the first line to the last without ever attaining the rewarding feeling of having really understood the text. Only later did I realize that understanding is not so much a result as a process that never ends. And today I put aside the sort of book that gives everything away on the first reading.

Who knows, maybe I'll get past the stage of drowning in quantum physics too.

But, to avoid further complaints, I'll start today with your grandpa, who wasn't always as calm, meek and friendly as you remember him. When I was a child, I saw him angry, sometimes really furious. The walls shook when he shouted. Really!

Your grandpa shouted so loud the walls shook. That's how it seemed to me at any rate, whether he was shouting about me or one of your uncles, and likewise if he was having a disagreement with your grandma. Okay, Grandma was no slouch as a vocalist herself, only she didn't have anything like the belly volume to produce such deep, powerful, marrow-piercing, thundering sounds as your grandpa. Grandma's shouts were more like a shrill siren – which wasn't exactly musical either.

Today I think the fierce rows actually helped your grandpa's and grandma's marriage to last to the end – sixty-five years! The two of them had somehow found a way to communicate to each other their dark emotions too. That scared us children sometimes, and the neighbours too were not always happy about your grandparents' tempers. But after the storm, the calm always returned, and more than just calm: after an interlude of resentment, there was sincere reconciliation. They loved each other, and couldn't do without each other, although there were things about each of them that the other didn't like. By talking about it, and occasionally shouting about it, hurling their accusations with full force, they at least kept their resentments from smouldering away inside them.

That's how I see it today, although as a child I was very frightened when your grandpa and grandma fought, and I put my hands over my ears.

Why am I telling you this?

All right, that was another one of those rhetorical questions that only annoy you. But, in fact, I'm asking myself why I'm talking about my shouting father today.

I'm not sure exactly. I think I wanted to amend the image of the kind, humble and wise grandfather that I sketched yesterday. That picture isn't wrong, but it isn't complete either. And it won't diminish your love and respect if you learn that your grandpa had to grow into what he was in the end to you grandchildren. None of the saints that people revere was born a saint; every one of them had a long road to travel, and no doubt some wrong turns along the way; more than a few of them had been selfish, vain, even bellicose, before the goodness saturated them.

I don't want to make Grandpa into a saint – that he certainly wasn't, or if so then only in the very last days, when he made peace with death and drifted away from us. What I want to say is, it would feel dishonest to me to ignore a person's disagreeable or disturbing traits, even if it's my own father. And the same is true – ah, and now I know why I started telling you about Grandpa's temper – the same is true of a relationship to God.

This feeling that something's not quite right if the only image of Grandpa that remains is the last one, the humble, devout, kind old man, still smiling in spite of the pain – I got this feeling yesterday, strangely enough, about our book too: the picture of God that I'm teaching you suddenly didn't seem honest because I skimmed over the dark part too quickly. Although I hinted here and there that it's hard to come up with an explanation, much less a justification, for so much injustice, poverty, hunger, pain, I should have admitted that the evil in the world makes me doubt, time and time again, whether God is just. When I was just a little older than you, I doubted whether God even existed.

The polytheistic religions have an easier time of it: they have compassionate *and* resentful gods, and so they can interpret the way of the world as a struggle between different powers. But, more importantly, most other religions don't even raise an expectation that all is for the best on our little Earth here.

To them, order is on the cosmic level; peace reigns in heaven, justice is relegated to the afterlife, or the rewards and punishments for a person's actions are received on reincarnation. In Buddhism, for example, as I mentioned, the best you can hope for is not to be reborn. In Hinduism, a person is responsible for everything that happens to them – if they suffer, it is because they sinned in their past life.

Incidentally, that's the ethical basis of the caste system that we find so unjust: a person can never leave the social class they were born into, and an 'untouchable' is traditionally only allowed to practise the most despised occupations, such as cleaning latrines or disposing of carrion. The better your karma, the sum of all your good and bad deeds, the better off you are in the next life. If you're born into a low caste, you'll have enough opportunities, in the endless flow of time, to make up for your omissions so that someday you will belong to the highest caste, the Brahmans. But if you kick downward, you'll land at the bottom yourself. Now that doesn't sound quite so unjust – and yet Mahatma Gandhi, and many other Hindus along with him, fought against the caste system, so that it was abolished, officially at least, when India became independent in 1948. So, yes, in Hinduism too, it's complicated, for one thing because 'Hinduism' doesn't really exist: the British colonial administration introduced the term in order to put all of the Indians' different, overlapping, and to the British confusing, religious beliefs into one pigeonhole. The administrators were not exactly luminaries of religious studies.

In any case, it's very clearly we monotheists who have the bigger problem explaining evil. Because we not only have just one God Who is responsible for everything – but this God is also supposed to be compassionate and just. That leads to a contradiction that can't be resolved by logic alone: either God *can't* prevent suffering, in which case He is not omnipotent; or He doesn't *want* to prevent it, in which case He is not good. If

God is both good and omnipotent, there shouldn't be any evil
in the world. After all, He would have the power to prevent
children from starving; He would be dismayed to see refugees
in our prosperous Europe fenced into camps with nothing but
a plastic sheet over their heads, even in winter; His justice
would never allow bombs to fall on innocent, uninvolved civil-
ians in the many wars going on in the world – probably in this
very second, while I am thinking about God in my comfortable
study. And even here, right here in the neighbourhood where
we live in Cologne, there once lived many Jewish families – as
you can see by the gold-coloured blocks with their names on
them in the pavement – some of them in our building, and
maybe in our flat. Then, not even 80 years ago, not even a
lifetime ago, troops of armed officers kicked in the door and
carted father, mother, children away to be gassed because
the German state had declared them vermin. How could God
stand by and watch that happen?

Certainly, much, if not most, of the evil in the world could
be explained by the free will which God has granted to human
beings. But what about natural disasters, which have always
existed? What about diseases and epidemics, unbearable pain,
stillborn babies, or children born with disabilities? And why
did God make human beings capable of being wolves to their
fellow human beings in the first place?

Please don't tell me now, in your keenness to defend animal
rights, that wolves aren't evil. It's a metaphor! I'm well aware
that wolves, unlike human beings, are obliged to kill. And to
the lamb it makes no difference who eats it, except maybe that
in our industrial farms we take away its enjoyment of life as
soon as it's born, and in our industrial abattoirs we deprive it
of dignity in death. But a lamb wouldn't believe anyone is good
or compassionate anyway, neither a human being nor a wolf.
Unlike the Jews, Christians, Muslims, who firmly believe that
God is good, even though He wipes out whole nations with a
single deluge or drought.

Now I could present you with all kinds of theories with which the scholars have tried over the centuries to explain suffering, injustice, the distress of innocent people. Muslim theology in particular has confronted this question from the beginning, because the Quran is not content with the biblical claim that God created a good world – 'and, behold, it was very good' – and then came the Fall. No, the Quran claims that the world not only was perfect at its beginning, but is still perfect now and everywhere: we human beings only have to look carefully.

> You do not see in the Creation
> Of the Merciful any flaw;
> And turn your gaze! Do you see any crack?
> Then turn again your gaze, and again!
> Your gaze comes back to you
> All tired and dull.
>   Surah 67:3f.

The standard against which the Creator measures His work couldn't be higher: no trace of a flaw must there be, and human beings need only use their senses and their reason to recognize God in His wisdom. And the first Muslims did just that: they looked closely.

And guess what happened.

They found that God's Creation did contain some flaws – many flaws, in fact. They went to the lepers, for example, and asked aloud how the Most Merciful of the Merciful could permit so much suffering. Muslim theology began in the eighth century, some hundred years after the revelation of the Quran, with that very question: why is there injustice in the world if God is all-powerful? Starting from this question, religious philosophy developed in the mosques, madrasas, libraries, universities; and if I tried to list all the different, often contradictory, answers, you can be sure I wouldn't finish by lunchtime. And anyway, I'd be surprised if any of the answers satisfied you.

What's more interesting, I find, is that the Quran, the Bible and presumably every revelation contains doubt itself in one way or another. It is our own doubts that are expressed in stories, prayers, verses – most drastically in Christianity perhaps, where God Himself suffers and dies on the cross.

> Every soul will taste death.
> With good We test you and with evil,
> And to Us you shall be brought home.
>
> Surah 21:35

We think the holy scriptures tell us how the world should be. No: they show the world as it is, and indeed more profoundly, realistically, sometimes brutally, than we would like. That is why the scriptures are so often concerned with wars, cruelty, the suffering of innocent people, people being crucified for their belief, as has happened again recently in Syria, Iraq, Libya under the rule of the so-called 'Islamic State'. And that is why teachers and parents leave out many verses when they teach the scriptures to children. The verses of violence are adult content, you might say, and so people only quote those of other people's religions, so that their own looks nice and peaceful in comparison. When I was a child, for example, I didn't know that God gets angry in the Quran, or that He wants to 'cut the roots' of the unbelievers (Surah 8, verse 7). From my parents and my grandparents, I always heard only the gentle sound, the poetic allegories and the admonitions to be just and merciful. My image of the Quran wasn't wrong, but it wasn't complete either. Because the holy scriptures are as peaceful and as bellicose as the world.

Just think: even in peacetime, even in the greatest prosperity or in the moment of supreme happiness, in every moment

– and that includes this moment as I write, or as you listen –
we could slip, from one heartbeat to the next, into the most
ghastly situation imaginable. A brain aneurysm, and you're
paralysed or mentally disabled for the rest of your life. A phone
call, and I hear that your sister has been killed in an accident.
The pain and the helplessness can be so bad that all we want is
to die. We think the holy scriptures offer consolation, and in
many verses they do. But, most of all, they portray a world in
which people are in need of consolation.

We can ignore all the cruelty, turn off the news, close our
eyes to illness, poverty and desperation, even in our immediate
neighbourhood; we can limit our readings of the holy scriptures to the verses that are pleasant. Only the fear doesn't go
away when we silence it: the fear that filled us at the moment
of our birth, when we were wrenched into the bright light.
And the terror that everyone encounters gnaws its way deeper
into our soul if we refuse to look at it. Even for me, who am
not a Christian, human horror is expressed nowhere more
drastically, movingly, harrowingly than in Jesus Christ calling
from the cross, 'My God, my God, why hast thou forsaken
me?' For the question is not simply that of an individual, not
only the cry of a victim of injustice and violence. It is the question of every human being from the cradle on, when all is dark
and they are afraid that their parents have abandoned them.
It is the question of my earliest memory, of waking up in my
cot at night with an earache, until someone finally picked me
up. My loneliness seemed endless, although it probably only
lasted a few seconds. And Mary's grief, not only to Christians,
but to many Muslims too, is the greatest pain that exists on
earth: that of a mother, a father, who must bury their own
child. There is nothing the religions shut out; they absorb the
full breadth of human experience, reflect it and place it in
a higher context. They are a path on which the Creator and
His creatures let their emotions fly, the dark as well as the
bright.

Do you feel safe from Him in Heaven
That He won't open up the Earth under your feet
When it quakes?
Do you feel safe from Him in Heaven
That He won't loose a storm upon you?
Then you will know how I warned you.
Those before them denied too,
And how I reproached them!
Surah 67:16ff.

Well, what about Satan? you may ask me this evening. Doesn't Satan have something to do with evil too?

That's right, there's also Satan, the Devil, Beelzebub or Iblis.

I never found Satan very convincing, to be honest, from childhood on. Significantly, Islamic theology never took him quite seriously either, although the Quran mentions him more often than the Bible. After all, what could Satan do against a God Who is all-powerful? And who created Satan in the first place, if not God Himself? So, no: I wasn't about to let God put the blame on Satan!

Later, however, I came across a different Satan, a tragic one. I mean the Satan told about by the Sufis, the Islamic mystics. It says in the Quran, when God created Man and gave him power on earth, he commanded the angels to bow down before Man. So all the angels bowed down except one, except Iblis. Then God said:

'What prevented you from bowing down when I commanded
     it?'
'I am better than he', answered Iblis,
'You made me of fire, him of clay.'
'Down with you!' cried God,
'Pride does not behove you in Paradise.
Begone! From now on you are of the humblest.'
Surah 7:12ff.

The Sufis wondered what Iblis meant by thinking himself better than Man. And they hit on the idea that 'fire' signified his ardent love, and the feelings of human beings were as brittle as dried mud in comparison. And for that reason Iblis was the only one among all the angels who refused to obey God: out of love. He loved God so much that he couldn't bring himself to bow down before anyone else. For love of God, he brought God's curse upon himself; for love he was driven out of Paradise; for love he has wandered the earth, disconsolate, as Satan. To the Sufis, that makes Satan the most loyal in his faith, and even, as one put it, 'more monotheistic than God Himself'. Satan felt as if God had bound him and thrown him in the sea and then mocked him: Be careful you don't get wet.

The mystics' Satan offers no explanation of why there is evil. On the contrary, he himself is a victim of God's inscrutable decree, an innocent convict and a martyr for love. If he tempts human beings to do evil, it is out of jealousy, because God prefers them to the angels. Yes, this story about Satan says a lot about love, which is not always pleasant and fulfilled, but can also be destructive, unhealthy, too extreme. Families too don't always break up for lack of love between father and mother. With some parents, it's because there was too much love. Passion – ah! language is so wise – passion comes from pathos, suffering, not from happiness. Satan introduces us to the dark secret of love. He doesn't explain evil, perhaps because there is no explanation. Or can you think of one?

I'm sorry, today's chapter hasn't turned out much simpler than yesterday's. Maybe tomorrow I'll start over again with Creation.

If You Doubt, You Think

O kay, let's talk about the darkness a little longer, if it's on your mind; we'll get back to the glad tidings afterwards. Apparently, God wants us to doubt – otherwise, He would have told simpler, more agreeable stories. Because if you doubt, you think, and only a thinking person can approve of God's Creation with conviction. But you can only approve of something if you also have the option of disapproving.

Do you remember Abraham? God commanded him to kill his own son – his firstborn, Ishmael, according to the Quran, or his younger son, Isaac, in the Bible – commanded him to slaughter him with a knife like an animal. As a child, I could hardly bear hearing it. Then I didn't think about it any more for a long time, and only when I became a father myself, I realized once again that no command could be more cruel. And Abraham, revered as the patriarch of all the prophets by Jews, Christians and Muslims alike – Abraham obeys. He lays his son – no, he presses his son by main force – down on a block, and raises the whetted knife. Although an angel intervenes in the last second and stops the father from committing the murder, what was burnt into my soul is that he would have done it, would have slaughtered his own child, just because an inner voice commanded him. That's horrific! And yet Abraham is considered a prophet. Why?

I hesitate to give you my answer. Yes, I have struggled long with Abraham and read many of the explanations that have been written over the centuries. In the meantime, I've made my peace with his story, although I still think there is none more cruel in the Quran or the Bible. Only I don't want to give you answers – as an adult I tend to do that much too often; in this book, too, I'm sorry to say. Actually, I wanted to guide you to the questions that arise when you study God's revelation, whether in nature or the scriptures. We think the holy books give answers, but we don't notice that the answers we find in reading them are our own. No, the books raise questions – and the most urgent questions of our existence.

We happen to be surrounded by violence, suffering, death; wars in which children are sent to die for their fatherland, as Abraham's child was to die for a higher ideal. It's no coincidence that 'infantry' – the foot soldiers, who always sacrifice the most in a battle – contains the word 'infant'.

But nature too, which we rightly so often praise, every single leaf of our chestnut tree – put it under a microscope and you will find, even in a drop of water, nothing but a struggle for survival among single-celled predators and vegetarian protozoans. It's no different among insects, no different in the forest, no different in the sea, no different in the desert, no different in the sky. Did I say there was love between the sun and the flowers? That's right, but just as much a part of nature is the enmity between the wolf and the sheep. And the sheep in turn eats a thousand tiny animals along with the grass. The will to live is so strong, so unbridled, that every creature on earth kills without batting an eyelash. Even the plants, the meek little plants: the flowers mercilessly elbow each other out of the light; as years go by the vines strangle the trees they climb on; even the grass lives at the expense of inorganic, foreign matter. Every hunter is at the same time hunted, just as in the history of humanity the progress of one group has always been the disaster of others; you can run down the list of all the civilizations. Life itself is one big conflict, starting from the moment scientists now call the Big Bang and religion calls Creation, when out of One came Difference.

> Did they not see, those who deny,
> That Heaven and Earth were once a single piece,
> And We divided it
> And made out of the water everything that lives,
> And yet they do not believe?
> ### Surah 21:30

Abraham, who loves God and loves his son, is subjected to the worst conflict until the angel announces to him that there is redemption, reconciliation, and that God wants no such sacrifice from us. In other words, the story as I understand it for myself is not about the sacrifice of the son at all. It is the story of the abolition of human sacrifice: keeping faith with Heaven does not conflict with life on Earth, and a choice in God's favour must never again be a decision against a human being. Prophecy does not mean having a better character; it means seeing more. It means feeling the fate of all humanity in one single soul. 'If you knew what I know, you would laugh little and weep much', said Muhammad. And Abraham was not always what he ended up being to the Jews, Christians, Muslims, and perhaps he was not always a prophet, but became one after having been horrified at himself. Because he would have done it. In every soul there is such an abyss, and so it took an angel to make the man understand.

Now I've given you an answer of sorts – forgive me. But the trouble is you're not here while I'm thinking all this, and so I just babble on. The conversation that every book hopes to be won't take place until this evening, or later, in the minds of everyone who reads it – with approval, with rejection;

hopefully with attention. The Quran also directly addresses its believing and unbelieving listeners again and again: sometimes the Muslims, sometimes the Jews and Christians, sometimes the polytheists; and it interrupts itself with their possible or actual objections. That's how you can tell that even the divine revelation is not a monologue. God in the Quran swears about the rich Meccans, for example, at least as rudely as Grandpa did when he used to get angry, just like a heated discussion in which the other person keeps on saying the same stupid things. Or God scolds Muhammad because he was gruff to a blind man who had asked him for advice. And occasionally God even groans in annoyance:

> No one is as quarrelsome as human beings!
>
> Surah 18:54

We know from archaeological finds that, at the time the Old Testament was written, children were sacrificed for religious purposes. And when Muhammad received the Quran, the Arabs still buried newborn daughters alive just because they weren't sons. In Surah 81, which I quoted a few days ago, among other passages:

> When the sun shall be darkened,
> when the stars shall be thrown down . . .

this old, cruel custom is mentioned:

> when the buried infant shall be asked
> for what sin she was slain.

It is one of the great achievements of the religions that they gradually overcame human sacrifice and infanticide. The Feast of Sacrifice that the Muslims celebrate every year, Eid al-Adha, commemorates the principle that children shall no longer die for a higher ideal.

Now you may think such stories have nothing to do with us any more; they take place in a mythical past or are invented, and far removed from our reality. No, they take place today; I won't say every day, because they are extreme situations; but they happen all over the world, and not only in wartime.

I assume you're going to want an example now.

I'll give you one that happened just a few months ago. A man I know, a strongly believing Christian, and his wife were expecting a child. During a medical examination, part of what is called prenatal diagnosis, it was found that there was a 95 per cent chance that the baby would have severe mental disabilities. It would live, but with no expectation of ever learning to talk, much less living an independent life. Ninety-five per cent. In this case it was not God Who suggested to the parents to abort the baby, which already had a nose, mouth, ears, a heart, a character and a face. It was the doctors, it was their surroundings, most of their friends and relatives – all of whom had the parents' best interests at heart. But the couple, the parents, decided, after a long struggle, to accept the child in the hope of the 5 per cent chance – although it meant accepting the other 95 per cent probability too as God's inscrutable wisdom. And why? Because they could not reconcile making a decision about life and death with their faith. Like many people who knew them, I was dismayed. Then the child was born, and it was healthy.

This story is not the same as that of Abraham and his son. But the conflict that the parents were subjected to from one second to the next was just as great: whether or not their own child should live. And the parents experienced their salvation as no less miraculous.

Did you not see him who argued with Abraham
About his Lord
Because God had given him the kingship?
'It is my Lord', spoke Abraham,

'Who maketh to live and to die.'
'No, it is I', spoke the other,
'Who make to live and to die.'
'Then if God brings the Sun out of the East,' spoke Abraham,
'Bring you it out of the West.'
Then the denier was dumbfounded.

Surah 2:258

God too has a history – has become what He is today. Although He is one, the same always and everywhere, human beings change constantly, and with them their concept of their Creator. In earlier times, when people were immediately exposed to nature, to fate, they felt more strongly that God's light can also shine black – that is, darkly and menacingly. The Bible and the Quran tell about this; so does the Gospel, which at the same time is full of love. They point out that the endlessness all around us can also be darkness.

God! No God except He,
The Living, the Everlasting.
No slumber overcomes Him, nor sleep.
His is what is in the Heavens and what is on Earth,
And no one can intercede with Him
Unless God Himself permits.
He knows what is before and after,
But no one receives anything of His knowledge
Except by His will.
His throne towers over Heaven and Earth;
To guard them is no burden to Him.
He is the Supreme, the Mighty.

Surah 2:255

Many people today only want to see the good side of God, the friendly side. They don't notice how small that makes Him, how powerless. And how great human beings make themselves out to be when they relieve God of His responsibility. They treat Him like a nice old man gone soft and frail – if they don't pronounce Him dead altogether. And yet it is He who saves us from distress – and also makes our heart stop whenever He chooses. God is not old; He is not young; He will continue to be when none of us is left in existence. And no one even asks a favour of Him unless He Himself permits it. No one partakes of God's knowledge unless it so pleases Him. He is the Merciful, the Compassionate, but also the Majestic, the Powerful to Whom human beings submit, surrender; with Whom they make peace, even if His light is not always distinguishable from darkness.

But couldn't we just as well consider God the darkness, or say He has no qualities? Why the insistence that God is just? After all, nature, to which the Quran so often appeals, knows no good or evil, hasn't even a purpose. Nature has only the law of cause and effect – stark, merciless causality: one thing follows from another, from the beginning of the world to the end. Reverence for life, which children learn in any kind of upbringing, is unheard of in nature. Not to murder, not to steal, to love even an enemy – the highest commandments in human culture have no meaning in nature. For nature treats life as if it were the most worthless thing in the world. Its creatures have no choice but to torment each other, exploit and destroy each other, and all their battles together make up the balance of nature. It is human beings, and only human beings, who are able to distinguish between good and evil. We want to believe – we should believe – in good. Because if we thought God evil, there would be no morality on earth. Through humankind, and only through humankind, life becomes more than an end in itself: it becomes kindness, beauty, decency, knowledge, sacrifice, courtesy. God too needs us in order for the life He created to be sanctified.

God needs us – that sounds pretty presumptuous. A physicist would probably tap his forehead at me now, because to a physicist the Earth – the solar system, for that matter, or even the Milky Way – is little more than one small wave in the immense ocean of galaxies; and God is supposed to need us human beings, of all things? There are certainly less awkward ways to phrase it, but I've exaggerated here on purpose. For the belief in only one God not only implies that the world is a continuous story that began billions of years ago and will not end – we hope – any time soon: monotheism also puts humanity at the centre of Creation. From the Old Testament on, history seems to be a single dialogue, often a heated one, between God and humankind. Then, in the New Testament, God Himself becomes human. And in the Quran, human beings are elevated once more.

Tomorrow, I'll try to explain the position of humanity in the cosmos as illustrated by our position in prayer: why do we spread our forearms when we pray and curve our hands as if we were carrying a big sphere, a kind of medicine ball? You can think about that until tomorrow. For now, I'll give you just this preview:

Extra Advance Section on Tradition!

There are many possible explanations, of course, since no one thinks up and prescribes such a position, or any other ritual or tradition: rituals emerge over decades and centuries. And that is precisely the reason why most of them are so wise and intuitive: because they were not created by one single person – their development involved countless people; and because they weren't created in a single moment, but over the course of decades and centuries.

Rituals and traditions are, you might say, the result of swarm intelligence – that is, the ability of animals or people to expand their capabilities, without a leader but well networked – although not over the Internet, as people are today. The

Internet is so fast, it shows you what's current this minute. In the religions, and similarly in literature, we see what has remained current from the dawn of humanity down to the present: whether love, death, violence or forgiveness; whether bringing up our children or our relationship to our parents; the search for meaning or the cry for justice. Besides, what prevails on the Internet is mainly whatever is loudest, shrillest, most radical – whatever produces the most excitement and thus the most clicks. Rituals and traditions, on the other hand, evolve so slowly that no one even notices the individual changes. They also ensure that the word of God, which in itself is often brusque or abrupt if you open the Quran or the Bible at random, fits gently into day-to-day life.

How do they do that? you may ask.

It doesn't take any magic tricks; it happens almost all by itself: by people coming back again and again, without really noticing it, to the gentle, harmonious verses that are especially helpful, for example, while the religious swarm intelligence, although it doesn't deny the harsher statements, pushes them towards the back of the people's consciousness, and even sets them aside in teaching children. I mentioned yesterday that, as a child, I hadn't the slightest idea how many threats and curses the Quran contains, and I suspect you too in your Religious Education class won't have read the Book of Hosea yet, or the Apocalypse of John, in which God's words are not exactly friendly. Just as your grandpa passed over in silence the fact that thieves in the Quran get a hand chopped off, Christian parents don't specifically teach their children Jesus' statement that his followers must hate their father and mother. Traditions are how the divine truth is embedded in human day-to-day life, which can afford joy as well as tribulation.

Imagine a stone not carved with a chisel but lying in the river and shaped by the water over decades and centuries: a stone like that feels soft and pleasant in any hand, at all times. In the Internet, there are too many chisels; there the world is full of edges, rough surfaces and sharp breaks; yet reality – what we experience in real life – is often soft, illogical and diffuse. Each impression and experience flows into the next, like the flowing water, and we, like the British officials in India, often don't know whether a thing belongs here or there, which side is up and which is down. And the rituals and traditions are so well formed and so satisfying – an originally religious practice like yoga, or a certain position in prayer – because many different people from different times and cultures have come to a consensus about them. They reach beyond the necessarily limited mind of an individual person and a single time. And beyond this morning's writing session, too.

Everyone Is a Caliphess

Yesterday you raised an objection that kept me thinking overnight. You asked whether Abraham wasn't more aghast at God than at himself. At a God Who commanded him to sacrifice his own son. Having to lay his own son on the block must have been worse than any nightmare for Abraham – and worse still for Ishmael. How could a son ever trust his father again, or a person trust God?

People don't like to talk about 'sacrifice' any more. Even many Christians are unaware these days that their religion is based on a sacrificial offering, and the priest or the pastor in today's church rarely spells out in detail what the sculpture behind him represents – that is, that God had His own son nailed to a cross with rusty nails as thick as your finger, and let him hang gasping, three, four metres up in the air, for days, naked in the sun, tormented by the pain, the thirst, the fear of death and also the scorn that members of his own people shouted up at him. In newer churches, the martyrdom is not shown at all any more; the cross is there, but not the crucifix. And yet Christianity is about exactly that: a God Who lets His child die a cruel death. For someone to give up their life voluntarily for something – that alone would be called insane today, if not criminal. But their own son's life?

Of all aspects of religions, sacrifice makes the least sense to people today. To you, even the sacrifice of lambs at Eid al-Adha probably makes little sense – except maybe the distribution of the meat among the poor. But I too would rather not see all the blood that flows at a religious slaughtering because each animal's throat is cut individually with a knife, and not on a factory production line. But religion says, Look at the Cross. Look at the slaughtered lamb, look carefully. Look at the fact that life depends on destruction, and that every birth is the announcement of another death. Okay, maybe religion says that only to adults; the sacrifice was absent even from my upbringing; your grandpa and grandma hardly ever mentioned it. And yet it has been part of religion since its inception.

About a hundred years ago, Mahatma Gandhi, who led the Indians' non-violent resistance against British colonial rule, named the seven deadly sins of modern society. There was wealth without work, pleasure without conscience, knowledge without character – all of them more topical than ever today. Only one of the modern sins that Gandhi listed was not so well matched with the others: worship without sacrifice. Gandhi of all people, whose pacifism defeated the British Empire and whom we revere as one of the great political and spiritual figures of the twentieth century, Gandhi of all people said that worship is a deadly sin if it does not involve sacrifice.

What did he mean by that?

Think about that yourself first, and I'll give you my own answer tomorrow – or not, as you like.

In the meantime, I'll go back to the question from yesterday: what are we holding in our upturned hands, symbolically, when we pray with our back straight, our chest wide and our forearms spread? That's a self-assured position, you said yesterday. Christians usually pray quite differently: they fold their hands and bow their backs. You also noticed, when you gave it your attention yesterday, that in our prayer position you automatically become aware of your breathing. By now you know that God's spirit comes and goes in human beings, flows in and out, as we breathe. At the same time, your gaze is directed outward when you sit or stand upright; in other words, you perceive the world around you, which is full of signs. That also strikes me as a plausible explanation.

But do you know how Grandpa explained to me the Islamic attitude of prayer? He said, what we're carrying when we pray is the whole world. Because, in Islam, human beings are the caliphs of God – *khalīfa* in Arabic. Literally translated, that means 'the viceroy' or 'deputy', or the 'successor', of God. That is a small but very important difference from the Bible, as I later learned.

Let's open the Bible and the Quran side by side and compare the sentences about the creation of human beings. In the Bible, it says, in Genesis, chapter 1, verse 27: 'So God created man in his own image, in the image of God created he him; male and female created he them.' In the Quran, however, Surah 2, verse 30, God says, after He has created all the animals and plants on earth, and also the angels and the seven Heavens – God says: 'Behold, I will place a *khalīfa* on the earth', that is, a successor or deputy.

An image is something different from a successor or deputy. An image is someone who looks like God. A successor or deputy is someone who takes on God's duties. Do you see the difference?

Declaring human beings the deputies of God, and not just His image, entails a tremendous exaltation. When human beings become creators themselves – when they conceive, bear and raise a child, when they heal a sick person, feed a hungry person, save a drowning person, revive the spirits of a depressed person, or love another person – they are continuing God's work. But also when people write poetry, they are God's successors; when they compose, paint, play, explore, invent, discover – yes, when they plough, plant, build or bake, as long as they do it with devotion.

But it also entails a tremendous responsibility that God lays on human beings: it is no longer God, but humanity who hold the fate of the world in their hands. After all, you might think humans are just one more kind of animal. From a scientist's point of view, that would probably be more logical, and there are religions, and were among earlier peoples, in which human beings have no special status in Creation. That may make people feel still more connected with nature – for my part, anyway, I don't think it's far-fetched or intuitively wrong. But in Judaism, in Christianity and in Islam, human beings are singled out as a unique kind of creature: they are the only ones to which God delegated responsibility for the world.

Now you'll say, That didn't turn out so well, giving humans responsibility for the world. And do you know what? The angels were afraid it wouldn't, and you're an angel too in a way.

And when your Lord said to the angels,
'I will install a successor on the earth',
They said, 'Will You put someone on earth
Who will do mischief and spill blood –
When we sing Your praise and hallow You?'

Surah 2:30

God did not say the angels were wrong; He only answered: 'I know what you know not.' Then God taught the people the names: in other words, he taught them language, and with language, knowledge, cognition, abstract thinking.

Abstract thinking sounds complicated, I admit. But it basically means something very simple and ordinary. For example, now I say 'tree': you don't have to see a tree; the simple sequence of sounds T-R-EE is enough for you to understand what I mean. Your idea is abstract, which means you're not thinking in sensory perceptions, but in concepts, names.

You can say what you want about animals, but I think it is extremely unlikely that they have names for each other, or for us people. At the outside, a dog associates its master or mistress with their voice, or with a certain sound they use to greet the dog. But those are sounds that the dog's master or mistress makes. A name, on the other hand, is separate from the object it designates. The name of the dog is 'dog', not 'woof'; the name of the cat is 'cat', not 'meow'. And so on. Sure, there's the cuckoo, which is called that because its call sounds similar, but such names are rare, and the cuckoo itself probably has no idea that its name is 'cuckoo'. We gave you a name before we knew what you'd be like – and be glad, otherwise we might have named you 'Cheeky', or better yet 'No!', because it's the word you say most often. Or simply 'Our Greatest Joy on Earth', which is true, although it wouldn't be very apt in the classroom: 'Our Greatest Joy on Earth hasn't done her homework!'

After God had taught the people all the names, He told the angels to name things. Of course, the angels couldn't – not even the angels can do what human beings can: namely, use not only their understanding – which animals have too – but also their reason.

And now you probably want to know what the difference is between understanding and reason.

Well, when dark clouds cover the sky, our understanding tells us – just as that of the animals and the angels does – that it's going to rain. We can make that association based on our experience: dark clouds equal rain. Reason, on the other hand, tells us – but only us human beings, not the animals, not the angels – that the climate is going to become unbearable on earth in 30, 40 years if we keep pumping so much CO_2 into the sky. In other words, human beings, and only human beings, can reach with our minds beyond our own reality; we can transcend the world, to use the philosophers' term. Which means, literally, 'climb beyond'. And that's exactly what happens in science, in art and also in religion: human beings, and only human beings, transcend or 'climb beyond' the boundaries of their own immediate experience. They visit cemeteries to commemorate their dead, and they create works of art that outlive them by 15,000 years, if you think of the cave paintings in southern France. As historians, human beings look back to the dawn of civilization; as astronomers, they calculate billions of years ahead how the stars in the Milky Way will move.

Religious human beings do essentially the same thing, only in regard to being itself: from the facts, their experiences and the revelations of life, they infer what may be before and after. Animals are different: everything we know suggests that their being begins with their birth and ends with their death. To them, being and life are the same. It wouldn't occur to them to bury their dead, or to commemorate them on certain days. Animals are likewise unable to imagine something that outlasts them, to say nothing of God. Not even whales can do that, as far as we know, although whales are much more intelligent than human beings. Even ravens and dogs are supposed to be more intelligent than we are, I've read, although I can't believe our neighbour Norbert's beagle could be smarter than . . .

Oh, my God, I can already hear you shouting: Of course Norbert's beagle is smarter than you, Papa!

. . . so I'll say right off that I am not going to discuss it at all. A beagle can be as intelligent as it likes: it will still never consider whether I might step on the messes it leaves. If I, on the other hand, were to leave a mess, just hypothetically, on the pavement in front of our building, during the night, say, then I couldn't help worrying that someone might step in it the next morning.

Although, to be honest, if that stupid Norbert stepped in it that wouldn't be so bad, I don't think, having stepped in his beagle's messes often enough. But the point is, I think about the consequences of my acts: I imagine a young man, for example, who's on his way to meet his sweetheart, and is definitely at a disadvantage if his shoes stink of my leavings, or I imagine our neighbour Norbert, who has once again forgotten his little bag when he's walking his beagle, and no sooner opens the door than he steps in my fragrant muck. Because what I have – at least potentially, sometimes I doubt it myself – what every human being has, is reason. Reason is what makes us special in all of Creation. Our neighbours might step in the messes we leave. Our children and grandchildren will have to live on the Earth that we are abusing.

> The sun and the moon keep their orbits as designed,
> And stars and trees bow down in prayer.
> And God has raised Heaven and set up the balance.
> So do not violate the balance,
> And keep the weight right,
> And do not shorten the balance!
> Surah 55:5ff.

But there's another way to explain the difference between understanding and reason: as simply as the Bible and the Quran do. In the Semitic languages – the Hebrew of Moses, the Aramaic of Jesus and the Arabic of Muhammad – reason is located in the heart. Thus, reason would be understanding plus heart. Or an intelligent heart.

As a child I told your grandpa the angels were right when they warned God: human beings do so much mischief, so much blood is spilled senselessly in the world – all the wars, the poverty, the dictatorships and so on. Yes, that's true, Grandpa answered, but that seems to be the price of freedom: you can also use it for bad purposes. God put His trust in human beings; but human beings have rarely lived up to their responsibility for the world. That's why God sent all the messengers and revealed all the books to warn them and guide them to do right after all – Bible, Torah and Quran, and also the Indian Vedas, the Chinese Tao Te Ching and so on, to each people in their own language, appealing to us human beings not just to live from day to day, but to look beyond – transcend! – our own birth, our own death: to consider what was before us and what will come after us. In regard to the next life, that means conceiving our earthly existence as transitory. And in regard to this life, remembering our ancestors and caring for our posterity. Religious people see themselves as a single link in a chain that extends beyond their own lifetime, and beyond the lifetimes of all people, to eternity.

It's much too late for mere warnings, you may be thinking now.

No: if we believe the Quran, it's never too late to start the Creation over again, and we can trust that God will assist us. For God – remember! – is also just a word, an abstraction: God means the principle or the ground of all life, and hence of all love, for life arises from love – the love between man and woman, the love between sun and flower, the love between God and human beings, the love between parent and child everywhere in the animal kingdom. God is specifically not the principle or the ground of death, and hence of hate, for hate is not creative; hate only destroys. And if we human beings have His spirit in us, as the Bible and the Quran teach, the spirit of God and thus the principle of life, then we are in keeping with our own divine nature if we love rather than hating, and if we protect the world and create it anew every day instead of destroying it. That's what it means to say every one of us is a caliph, or, to be more exact, each of us *should be* a caliph – we should act in our own lives as though we bore responsibility for all of Creation. And, to be still more exact, we are not caliphs, but caliphesses.

Why do you say that? you will probably ask now (I imagine, in my God-given faculty of reason).

Because, oddly, the Arabic word *khalīfa* is feminine. The masculine form would be *khalīf*, but it doesn't exist in the language, surprisingly. A caliph in Arabic is always a caliphess, even if it's a man. Linguistically, that's a very unusual situation in Arabic. It's as though in English you had to call any man who becomes prime minister 'Madam Prime Minister'. Or say that Colin Firth was a brilliant actress. Or if all teachers, whether men or women, were called schoolmistresses. Weird, isn't it?

Why it is that a caliph is always a caliphess, I don't know; in reality, all the caliphs have been men, and women rulers in the Arabic-speaking world have been very rare. Apparently the language, because it is formed over countless generations, is smarter – swarm intelligence, you know – than the individual speaker. And if you consider that it's the women who bear the children, and are thus creators like God, then maybe it would be good if we, as vicaresses of God on Earth, loved this Creation as much as a mother loves her own child.

Jesus' Wisdom

You seem to be quite preoccupied with sacrifice to be asking about it again and again. It appears to be troubling you, or at least unsettling you. I can be glad Islam is content with the sacrifice of a lamb, and I don't have to get you to accept the Crucifixion. And, in any case, I sometimes think God sent Muhammad because He Himself noticed that the duties He places on human beings with Christianity are too burdensome: duties of understanding, duties of faith, duties of the heart. Because it's not just the monstrosity that God allows His own son to die a cruel death – an 'offence', as the Bible itself calls it. The Eucharist too is an event that is very difficult to grasp, much less explain to a child: you eat and drink the body and blood of your Lord. And, last but not least, loving your enemies: that's very difficult even for individuals to practise; as an ideal for a whole society, it would be mad – should the Aztecs have loved the Spanish conquistador Cortés, who exterminated them, or the Jews have blessed Hitler, aided and comforted him and prayed for him, as the Sermon on the Mount advises? And I'd like to see the father who would ask his child to turn the other cheek when someone hits him or her in the schoolyard. I'd alert the child protection services.

Loving your enemies can be understood in a figurative sense at best: meaning, for example, that you are kind not only to your friends, relatives, neighbours, like-minded people or members of your ethnic group, but also to other groups, foreigners, people of different opinions, opponents – and that you still see, in the most annoying teacher, the meanest exploiter, the most obnoxious politician, the child they once were, the dying person they will one day be. As a writer, what I understand as loving my enemies is this: that I try to give expression to the incomprehensible, the foreign, the obscure – what I don't understand, what is unfamiliar, what is dark in my own psyche and in the world. A state can translate love for its enemies into laws to ensure that even the terrorist who fights the state enjoys fundamental rights. However, that has taken almost 2,000 years, and, especially these days, people increasingly question fundamental rights, in Europe and elsewhere.

Islam makes it easier for a father, because he basically has to tell his children only this: Look around you, respect the order of nature, the animals' will to live, your own instincts, which are right. Always strive for peace, but if you are attacked, you may defend yourself. Our Prophet seems to me altogether more realistic and far more pragmatic than his predecessor Jesus, who was inspired (or inspirited) by love to the roots of his hair. What Jesus asks of us is beautiful, but also radical and sometimes enigmatic: we're supposed to love our enemy; we're supposed to turn the other cheek when someone hits us; we're supposed to tear out our eye and cut off our hand if they tempt us to sin. Of course, that's not to be taken literally, and perhaps becomes more understandable upon reflection, yet even so, it is strong stuff: tearing your own eye out – whew! Muhammad's precepts are perfectly simple in comparison – his most famous piece of advice, for example: 'Trust in God, but tether your camel.'

That's not a superficial statement by any means; it contains a deep wisdom: namely, that our trust in God does not relieve us of our own responsibility, and only both in conjunction will grant us a devout serenity. Nevertheless, we can also understand the sentence in its immediate sense, with applications in practically every situation, from exams and competitive sports to relationships and cancer treatments, to crises of faith and even politics. 'Trust in God, but tether your camel.'

Of course, there are a few specific commandments in Islam too; they're not so hard to follow, though: bearing witness to God and His Prophet; prayers five or three times daily; fasting during Ramadan; alms to the poor; making the trip to Mecca, if you can.

> Serve your Lord, and do good,
> That you may prosper.
> And struggle, struggle for God;
> He has chosen you,
> Has laid nothing difficult on you in religion.
>
> *Surah 22:77f.*

And if you, native of Cologne that you are, don't want to renounce your glass of Kölsch when the whole city is celebrating Carnival, God explicitly cuts you some slack.

> Say: 'O my servants who have transgressed against your own
>   souls,
> Do not despair of God's mercy!
> God forgives sins altogether;
> Indeed He is the Forgiver, the Merciful.'
>
> *Surah 39:53*

Haven't you ever noticed, when we've visited him in Isfahan, that even your great-uncle Ebrahim, who never misses a prayer, still drinks his vodka every evening? Lots of our relatives, if not most, in fact, used to be like Uncle Ebrahim: they observed the religious commandments, not the way a soldier obeys a command, but more the way you obey your father: when I say you have to get to sleep by ten at the latest, there's hope you'll be in bed by eleven. And just like you offering to eat an apple if you're allowed to stay up later, they haggle with their God: Let me nibble on the sausage at our Armenian neighbours' house today, and I'll add an extra scoop to my alms.

> Against those who believe and do good works
> No sin shall be charged for whatever they eat,
> As long as they are godfearing and believe and do good works,
> And then are godfearing and believe,
> And then are godfearing and do good;
> God loves those who do good.
>
> Surah 5:93

And yet there is a truth in the cross that is older than Christianity: God dies for humanity's sake in many pre-Christian cultures – in Babylon for example, and in ancient Persia. The Muslims too, although they deny the Crucifixion, have returned again and again to martyrdom – that is, death as sacrifice – the Sufis especially, and in a different way the Shiites, who make up the majority of Muslims in Iran. For the Shiites, eleven of the twelve imams, the successors of the Prophet, were murdered because they stood for justice, the poor and the truth. Only the twelfth Imam, the Mahdi, disappeared before he could be killed, and will return at the end of the world, like Jesus Christ. Some say that the Mahdi is none other than Jesus Christ himself.

Although we may never understand it completely, we feel that there is a mystery in martyrdom, the greatest possible sacrifice that a person can make. We feel that trust in God alone is not in keeping with human experience. Because human experience includes that of trust being broken. Jesus' complaint that God had forsaken him was David's complaint in the Old Testament, and will continue to be the complaint of everyone who is oppressed, tormented or overwhelmed with suffering on earth. And the Resurrection salvages the hope that the sufferers will find justice in the next life.

Thus, many Sufis have experienced not only Muhammad's wisdom, but likewise Abraham's wisdom, Noah's wisdom, Salomon's wisdom, Joseph's wisdom, but most of all, Jesus' wisdom – in Arabic: *al-ḥikma al-ʿisawīya* – and followed Christ's way even up to the cross. 'What is love?' the famous mystic al-Hallaj was asked in the tenth century in Baghdad. 'You will see it today and tomorrow and the next day', answered al-Hallaj. But the same day, they chopped off his hands and feet; the next day they hanged him; and on the third day they scattered his ashes in the wind.

Enough of this! I'm not sure, to begin with, whether I'm not confronting you with the topic too early – I'm sure your grandpa would have protested, and, besides, you've already gone further in your own reflections: yesterday you said Gandhi didn't meditate all day long, he risked his life again and again for his political goal. And that you could very well see a meaning in the sacrifice a person makes for others. After all, the purpose is not to make ourselves better off; it's to make the world better. And, yes, you're probably right that a better world won't be possible without giving up something, without sacrifice. We will not succeed in saving the climate, ending the misery of refugees, ensuring more justice in the world if we in the wealthy countries only want to keep buying more, owning more, being more comfortable. Today, more than ever, when religion is often presented as a feel-good proposition – alongside spas, neighbourhood centres and t'ai chi – Jesus, the twelve imams and al-Hallaj remind us that the objective is not personal fulfilment. The objective is to perfect yourself so that you can serve others. I can understand that you still have trouble accepting the slaughtering of lambs at Eid al-Adha. You don't even eat meat any more.

End of the Discussion of Sacrifice, for Now!

Today I'd like to call your attention to another difference between Christianity and Islam, illustrated by one and the same story told in both the Bible and the Quran. I said before that the properties of a religion only become really significant when you compare it with another religion, ideally the nearest neighbour – that tiny fraction of difference! In your Religious Education lessons, I'm sure you've heard that human beings have been born with original sin since Adam and Eve's transgression – the 'Fall of Man'. Eve, tempted by the serpent, persuades her husband Adam to eat of the tree of knowledge which God has forbidden them; they are both driven out of Paradise, and since then there has been sin in the world. In other words, the thirst for knowledge that your parents, teachers, books and educational television shows have tried to encourage since you were little – this innate faculty unique to human beings – is at the same time a danger, perhaps the greatest danger. If we had never wanted to know anything, we would still be in Paradise.

The idea that human nature is supposed to be sinful sounds at first absurd to Muslims – in Islam, after all, people are born good. But then, remember the angels in the Quran who warned God against appointing human beings, endowed with reason, as his deputies. Of course, there are natural disasters, people are subject to severe illnesses and die long before their time. Nonetheless, most of the afflictions, the worst destruction and the greatest injustices on earth are man-made: wars, tyranny, lies, villainy, violence. And they can all be traced to the fact that human beings are not content with what they possess by nature: for one thing, they are not content with the knowledge necessary for survival. Human beings strive for progress, for possessions, for knowledge, and also for power, from the discovery of fire to the Industrial Revolution, from the first migrations to the exploration of Mars. As you will read in Goethe's *Faust* (I hope) when you get to high school, progress, although it brings so many blessings – equality, medicines, heating and the abolition of human sacrifice – is at the same time a pact with the devil. The discovery of the chemical elements, which gave us modern medicine, which in turn gave your grandpa a peaceful death, has also allowed us to make poison gas and plastic waste.

Today, in fact, we live in an age in which humanity for the first time has the ability to wipe itself out, or to destroy the natural resources it needs to live. And evidently the capacity for evil is innate in human beings. Just think of what happened 80 years ago here in Germany, including our city, perhaps in this very building in which we live so comfortably today. Look at the wars that follow one after another without a break and are raging even now, the genocides, the crimes. Look at Cain and Abel, who were the very first siblings – and what happened? One of them killed the other.

Christianity thus draws a pessimistic picture, although you might also say a realistic one, of humankind. After all, God Himself, in the person of Jesus of Nazareth, was condemned by citizens, captured by soldiers, killed by hangmen, who at home were probably good family men, or who mourned their fathers just as I did mine. In Christianity, human beings need redemption, that is, a divine intervention, in order to escape damnation: their motives are by nature bad, and, whatever they do, even a saint, even someone who devotes his whole life to the poor, is dependent on divine mercy for salvation. And that goes not only for individual human beings, but for humanity collectively, who must wait for Jesus Christ to return when the earth finally collapses.

In other words, the destruction is actually inevitable, and we must hope for a miracle if the human race is to survive. But that miracle, if you read the Revelation of John metaphorically, would be Jesus Christ in human beings themselves, who must fall so low before they finally understand. Wherever we fight for good, for peace, for the environment, for justice in the world, wherever we give our possessions to the poor or sacrifice ourselves for our neighbour, the Redeemer – which Jesus is in Islam too – is probably at work in us. Or else God Himself is.

That is more or less how I, who am not a Christian, understand the picture that Christianity paints of human beings. If someone should say to you that Man is seen quite differently in Christianity, point out to them that they too are only giving you a single opinion, which is contested in turn by other Christians. Every religion is a bundle of possible answers, some of them mutually exclusive, to the questions that arise from God's revelation. And I think the scriptures deal with issues that are too important, and simply too gripping, to be the property of just a certain group. You don't need to be a Christian to learn something in Catholic Religious Education, just as the Quran doesn't speak exclusively to Muslims. You will get a few more of the answers, curious ones perhaps, that human beings have come up with. Conversely, a Christian too may get to know his or her own religion better the more they learn about other religions. Every journey, every real journey, whether through books, meetings or faraway continents, is at the same time a journey to yourself. Sometimes, though, you don't come back. It's too late today to start on Islam, because you'll be at the door any minute now. I'll save how Islam sees human nature for tomorrow.

While the rice is cooking, though, I'd like to bring something else to your attention, something fundamental which hasn't received the space it deserves in this book because here I'm thinking more about God than about how human beings should behave: Religions are not ends in themselves. They are never just about the individual's relationship to the endlessness that surrounds us, and to the endlessness inside him or her. At the same time, they are always about the individual's relationship to the community, and each of these relationships involves the other. That is why the highest stage of enlightenment is not being filled with God, enraptured, blissful. In almost all religions and especially in the mystical traditions, the highest stage was and is to turn again from that enlightenment towards human beings and to serve them, to be there for them, to love them indiscriminately. In other words, an enlightened person is someone for whom devotion to God and devotion to their fellow human beings are the same thing. An example in Islam of a person who has attained such perfection, and to many Sufis the very embodiment of human perfection, is Jesus Christ. Here you can see very clearly the distinction between the Christian Jesus and the Islamic – or, to be more precise, the Sufi – Jesus: to the Christians, Jesus is altogether unique as someone who is at the same time God and human. To the Sufis, Jesus stands for an ability that every human being has: the ability to develop their own divine nature. This too, and especially this, is part of the *ḥikma ʿisawīya*, the Wisdom of Jesus: that you, like Jesus, can become the spirit of God – filled with His spirit. You can find the paradigm of the human being attaining godhead in other religions too, though: in the Buddha, for example, or in Lao Tse.

Extra Section on the Difference between Christian and Islamic Architecture!

In Christianity, the uniqueness of Jesus as God's son is even carved in stone – just look for it the next time your school has a church service. To start with, the floor plan of a cathedral is modelled after the body of Christ on the cross: with the nave as the torso and legs, the transept as his outstretched arms, and the rounded apse at the end of the church as his head. When you walk into the church, you can easily see that the whole building is oriented towards the one and only place where God appears on earth, and thus the architecture reproduces human beings' movement towards God, along a long aisle from the outside world to the altar, where the light comes down in a steep angle from above. A mosque, on the other hand, has no central point. From every spot, the worshipper looks up into the cupola above, like the vault of heaven. In other words, the mosque is not designed to reflect the appearance of God at a certain place, at a certain time, in a singular person – but to communicate the fact of God's presence everywhere. That is why the worshippers in a mosque, no matter where they sit, stand, or bow down before God, are surrounded by the same circle, with no corners or edges to block their view. And the walls are decorated all around with perfectly shaped ornaments that mean nothing, show nothing, have no end and no beginning, because they symbolize the endlessness of God.

And one more thing: because God in Christianity became a human being – that is, something visible – you see pictures everywhere in Christian art: pictures of people, pictures of animals, pictures of nature. For that reason, Christianity is also called a visual culture, and has brought forth all the great painters. Because God in Islam became the Word – a recitation or a chant, to be exact – Islamic culture was for a long time an auditory culture, one of music, recitation and poetry, as well as of calligraphy. And so on and so forth . . . it is impossible to understand cultures without their roots in religion, and that most certainly goes for German literature too, or classical music – whether you yourself happen to be a believer or not.

End of the Extra Section on the Difference between Christian and Islamic Architecture!

To the Sufis, though, Jesus is not only the paragon of a human being completely filled with God. He is also an ethical model. Simply loving your neighbour is nothing particularly biblical or Quranic; it is taught in all religions in one way or another. The new idea that came into the world together with the belief in just one God is a different one, a social one – perhaps the most revolutionary idea in the history of humanity: all people are equal. You may think that goes without saying, but it is not to be taken for granted, neither in the world religions nor in world history, much less in relations between the sexes. Even the Greeks, whom we credit with the invention of democracy, would have thought it absurd that all people should be equal: their democracy was built on the labour of slaves making citizens free – and only male citizens, mind you. Only with the belief in a single God Who created the world did the idea of equality gradually expand to include all human beings, until the European Enlightenment and the French Revolution in the eighteenth century finally proclaimed political equality: *Liberté, égalité, fraternité*, the founders of the first French Republic demanded – freedom, equality and brotherhood.

It is a long time since we have needed God in order for people to enjoy equal rights, no matter what their sex, their birth, their religion, their age or their health, no matter what their social class or their sexual orientation – at least before the law. But that doesn't mean we should forget where the idea comes from that human dignity is inviolable, and what strength it still takes, and sometimes religious faith, to love not only your neighbour – that's almost natural, after all – but also your enemy, as Jesus taught. Because precisely that, loving your enemy, is the Christian extension of the monotheistic law of equality.

Now, at the beginning of the chapter I said, to us in Europe today, 'enemy' no longer means our adversary on the battlefield, but everyone who doesn't belong to our own family, community, language, nation: the foreigner, the misfit or the dissident. And 'love' in our society doesn't mean you're supposed to take every idiot into your heart, but to respect them as a person with equal rights, even – and especially – if they espouse opinions you disagree with, if they have done you wrong, or if they support Bayern Munich. The constitution translates 'love your enemy' into fundamental rights, from the right to bodily integrity to the rights to free speech, free exercise of religion, and political asylum. In religion, of course, love is indeed meant literally. 'The saints are like the earth,' the Islamic mystics teach, 'they do not return the stones we throw at them, but offer us flowers instead.' That doesn't just sound like the Sermon on the Mount: it is Jesus' commandment – in Islam.

But now I've rambled on again.

So if the rice is burnt, you'll offer me a flower anyway, won't you? And in reward, for dessert, you get a taste of Paradise, better than milk and honey: strawberries, chocolate sauce and vanilla ice cream. Even Paradise caters for your taste.

Will and Knowledge

How come only 'brotherhood'? you complained yesterday; how come the French revolutionaries didn't say anything about sisterhood?

Well, in those days, before the women's movement, 'brotherhood' was understood as meaning solidarity among all people. You could rewrite the motto about *liberté, égalité*, but French doesn't have a neutral word for 'siblings'. Even *fratrie*, 'siblinghood', shows the same descent from Latin *frater*, 'brother', as *fraternité*. And adding a word – *liberté, égalité, fraternité et sororité* – would sound like a call to divide sisters and brothers rather than unite them!

You notice straightaway that language brings its history with it – you can't have one without the other. But there is another reason why I don't think we should simply correct old texts wherever they exclude or offend someone. Because our understanding is just as limited as the understanding of our forebears, and in a few years the next amendment will be due, and another soon after that, and another and another, until someday nothing is left of the magic of the original, albeit old-fashioned, wording. But, most of all, an idea loses its usually painful history if we rephrase it for every period.

It is a fact of modern history, and European history in particular, that many people have not been treated equally; after all, there was colonialism, the slave trade, Auschwitz, genocides against the Native Americans, Hereros, Armenians, Tutsis, and so many more massacres, down to very recent times. But the idea of a united humanity shone even in the darkest days of politics. It gradually became separated from religion, and had to be defended against religion again and again, until it finally resulted in the Universal Declaration of Human Rights, which has been ratified by almost all states in the world. Since then, humanity has had, if not justice, then at least a binding guideline accepted on every continent, in every culture. This doesn't have very much to do with our topic. So you can complain to the French Republic about their motto, or go into politics yourself when you grow up, but now let me finally start my chapter, if you don't want to find yourself with no lunch.

Because it's not so easy to write a book, I'm discovering, when you bury me in questions every evening. I hardly dare say 'burp' because then you'll want to know what a burp is made of. And if I explain it, you'll checkmate me by saying that means a burp is also a kind of spirit!

No, seriously, I'm glad you ask questions. Some of them we deal with straightaway; others I ignore, or I hope the answers will come up by and by as we go on. But still, over and over again, you've raised objections that send me back to the drawing board, or that I have to sleep on. Yesterday, for example . . .

. . . Oh God, now I'm the one digressing . . .

. . . yesterday, when I said the Bible speaks not only to Jews or to Christians, you said, Don't we generally understand a thing better when we look at it from the outside than when we're caught up inside it? I thought that was an intriguing idea, and yes, I think you're absolutely right in some cases. If we have time at the end of this chapter, I'll give you an example of a Christian who understood Islam more accurately than almost all Muslims. But first, let's go back to the Fall again!

Beginning of the Chapter Proper!

The Quran has a more optimistic view of human nature than the Bible, whether rightly or not.

> It is God who made you the Earth for a settlement
> And the sky as a canopy;
> And gave you your shape, a beautiful shape,
> And provided you with good things.
>
> *Surah 40:64*

In general, Islam – no cross, no guilt, and all's right with the world – strikes me as a life-affirming, perhaps all too optimistic religion, as absurd as that may sound today, when our religion tends to be associated with violence and bigotry. And in Shia Islam, I admit, there is altogether too much weeping over the martyrs. So it's complicated in Islam too, and, to be exact, statements such as 'Islam is this' and 'Christianity wants that' are impossible, because the world religions are also the opposite of anything you can say about them. None of them contains a logical theory, an all-purpose textbook or a system of universally acknowledged statements. The Islam I'm trying to communicate to you is also only one possibility, and would be rejected by many, probably even most, Muslims today. Conversely, those Christians whom I revere – Francis of Assisi for example, or in our time Father Paolo Dall'Oglio, who was kidnapped in Syria – are not necessarily representative of Christianity. And for us there is the further complication that Islam has no such institution as the church to determine what is correct and what is incorrect. So I only follow my ancestors, teachers and models, the books on my shelves and, not least, the faculty of reason that has its seat in the heart.

Let's read Surah 20 together, starting at verse 116, where God drives the human beings out of Paradise:

When We said to the angels,
'Bow down to Adam',
They bowed; only Iblis refused.
'O Adam,' We said, 'behold,
This is an enemy to you and to your wife.
See that he does not expel you both
From the Garden and make you miserable.
For here you shall not hunger nor feel naked;
You shall not thirst nor suffer the heat of the sun.'
Then Satan whispered to him,
'O Adam, shall I take you to the Tree of Eternity,
And a kingdom that will never fade away?'
So the two of them ate of the Tree,
And became ashamed of their nakedness,
And they began tying leaves of the garden
Upon themselves.
Thus Adam disobeyed his Lord, and erred.
Then his Lord chose him,
And turned again to him, and guided him.

What is different in this version of the Fall from the story as told in the Bible?

First, it is not the Tree of Knowledge that God has forbidden Adam and Eve, but the Tree of Eternity. In other words, it is not the faculty of cognition that is declared dangerous, but rather the desire to live forever and be all-powerful – that is, to become like God.

Second, it is not the woman who tempts the man, as it is in the Bible, but the other way round.

In Surah 7:20ff., you can find the same story told again, somewhat differently:

Then Satan whispered to them
To reveal their nakedness, which had been hidden from them,
'Your Lord', he said, 'has only forbidden you this tree

Lest you become angels or become immortals.'
And he swore to them, 'I am a good advisor to you!'
So he tempted them by deception.
When they tasted of the tree
They became ashamed of their nakedness,
And they began tying leaves of the garden
Upon themselves.
And their Lord called to them: 'Did I not forbid you that tree,
And say Satan is evidently your enemy?'
'Our Lord,' they said, 'we have sinned against ourselves,
And if You do not forgive us and have mercy on us,
We shall be truly lost.'

The guilt falling on both Adam *and* Eve is typical of the Quran, which is called misogynistic nowadays: the Quran was, as far as I know, the first book ever – the first text in the Arabic language at least – to designate men and women explicitly, even though the convention in Arabic, as in other languages, is that the masculine form includes both sexes. In other words, the feminine form is used additionally in the Quran in places where it would not be grammatically necessary. That alone was a tremendous provocation in the seventh century. Furthermore, the Quran is the first Arabic text that accords women any rights at all. Not equal rights – women inherited only half of what men would, for example, and their testimony in court was worth less than that of men – and yet it was such an innovation at that time on the Arabian peninsula that even Muhammad's own companions protested. Unfortunately, after Muhammad's death, the men had the last word, as everywhere in the world, and they showed little interest in pursuing the emancipation that the Quran had begun. Some Islamic countries even backslide to the time before Muhammad, and, in most mosques, women's view of the endless circular space is blocked by curtains. Something similar can be said of the few penal provisions that the Quran contains, such as the rule that thieves should have a hand chopped off: it was progress in comparison to pre-Islamic times to have a legal system that applied to every person, regardless of their background, their tribe and their social status. Still, if laws are transferred one-to-one from the seventh century to the present day, they can only be cruel and archaic.

But to come back again to the Fall: there is another important difference from – no, not from the Bible itself in this case, but from a Christian tradition which reads something into the Bible that the scripture doesn't say in so many words. Although Adam and Eve are driven out of Paradise in the Quran too, their sin is not hereditary, as it is in Christianity. On the contrary, in the very next verse they are explicitly forgiven, and God turns towards them again in mercy.

'In the Earth shall be a place for you to settle
And a livelihood for a time.'
Surah 7:24

And so human beings in the Quran are born good, and belief in God is inherent in human nature. They not only have eyes, ears, a mouth, but are also endowed with reason. If they only look, they will recognize God's work all around them. However, people can also reject God's grace, as the surah further recounts:

Children of Adam! We have sent down garments
To cover your nakedness and adorn you.
But the garment of righteousness –
That is better; that is one of God's signs;
Maybe they will think on it.
Surah 7:26

That is the critical clause: 'Maybe they will think on it.' While Christianity emphasizes human beings' free will – that is, their drive to possess more, rule more, learn more – Islam focuses on the cognitive faculty. Seek knowledge, in China if need be, said the Prophet – China in those days was as far away as the moon is to us. The human will leads away from God; knowledge leads towards God: this is true in both religions – probably in all of them – but they differ in their emphasis. 'God has created nothing more noble than the cognitive faculty', the Prophet also says, 'and His wrath falls on those who disdain it.' That is why Islam has no such sacraments as baptism, confirmation, communion, matrimony, holy orders or extreme unction – that is, symbolic acts through which the grace of God is granted; Islam also has no priests to mediate between God and human beings, no miracles, no supernatural doctrines – in fact, strictly speaking, no dogmas at all, in the sense of doctrines to be followed absolutely, except the profession of faith itself, the *shahāda*: There is no God but God, and Muhammad is His messenger. In Islam, a person has his or her salvation, and humanity has its salvation, in their own hands.

> Whatever good befalls you is from God;
> Whatever evil befalls you is from yourself.
>
> Surah 4:79

Nothing stands between God and human beings; nothing keeps them from believing; and if someone commits an outrage, if they murder, steal, lie or fail in their responsibility for Creation, they are turning away. They are giving up their natural, innate attitude and sinning against themselves. Infants who cannot yet speak, children growing up, adults who use their senses and their reason are turned towards God. Unbelief is an act; belief on the other hand is the innate condition.

> Turn your face now to religion:
> Right faith is a gift
> With which God created humankind.
>
> Surah 30:30

In this light, the revelation of the world adds nothing new, strictly speaking, but only reveals a person's own divine nature: a person recognizes himself, herself. And that is why God says to the angels that He has created human beings perfect in form, and breathed His own spirit into them. In other words: Jesus, in Christianity a unique being, God become human, is in Islam the model of an ability inherent in every one of us. Although only very few people are completely filled with God – that is, with love for all creatures – the potential is within each one of us. And so 'ordinary' people such as Ibn Arabi or Francis of Assisi, Mahatma Gandhi or Martin Luther King, people who did not found new religions, nonetheless transcended themselves. The first human being – 'Adam', translated, means simply 'human being' – in Islam, the first human being is not a sinner, but a prophet.

> We created human beings from a drop,
> A mixture, to test them;
> And We gave them hearing and sight.
> We guided them on the way,
> Whether they are grateful or ungrateful.
>
> Surah 76:2f.

You said yourself, yesterday evening, that you just can't get it into your head that human beings could be sinful from birth, as Christianity has it.

Actually, a Muslim father may be glad to hear that. But your Catholic Religious Education teacher might rebut me with the opposite question, which makes a certain amount of sense: Is a child's soul really as pure as Islam teaches?

As a child, I at least was anything but an innocent lamb, and you too will remember one piece of wickedness or another that you inflicted on others, or suffered at the hands of some child, even in kindergarten. Even Jesus, human perfection incarnate, hurt his parents by running away during their visit to Jerusalem, when he was 12 years old, the same age as you. For three days, they looked for him desperately! And when they finally found him in the temple, and his mother asked how he could do that to them, he answered only with a rhetorical question: Why hadn't she known where he was?

Certainly, your Religious Education teacher will be able to interpret the passage in the Gospel of Luke (2:41–52) in some way that puts Jesus in not quite such an unfavourable light. But perhaps the Bible is more honest than many Christians give it credit for. And if I imagine we had been desperately looking for you for three days in a big, strange city, only to hear an insolent answer from you that shows no empathy at all – then I think even Jesus had a certain prior history before he became filled with love for all creatures. Luke himself reports at least that, after the episode in the temple, Jesus 'increased in wisdom and stature, and in favour with God and man' – so he did not have all this from birth. And what do you think the temptation of Jesus was about? Satan pestered him for forty days. Do you think Satan had horns and a fiery tail? No, Satan was in Jesus – in Jesus himself, no less – and even after the forty days, the fiend left him only 'for a season' (Luke 4:13).

A human being is – no, not an animal; he, or she, is lower than an animal once the demonic in him or her is unchained. Only human beings kill out of pure malevolence. The cat that torments a captive mouse has no capacity to feel compassion. Human beings on the other hand must weed out their compassion in order not to feel empathy with others. Wait until you're grown up: then you too will learn to suppress your commiseration when you hear in the news of refugees drowning again, or when you see homeless people in front of your door even in the bitterest winter. Otherwise, you wouldn't be able to sleep at night. And so human beings numb themselves, almost by necessity, just so their day-to-day lives can go on. Myself included.

So is Christianity right after all?

Maybe the biblical and Quranic ideas of human nature are not mutually exclusive. In the Bible too, Heaven is inside us; in the Quran too, there are verses in which human beings seem to be lost without divine intervention. I have told you about the different religions' tendencies, about the signposts that mark various points in the history of religion. Go ahead and think yourself about which image of human nature best portrays people of today. Do they need redemption, or do they have peace in their own hands? God Himself seems to have His doubts, or perhaps He is disappointed:

> To the Heavens and the Earth and the mountains
> We offered the trust to keep,
> But they refused to take it on,
> And were afraid of it.
> Then the human beings took it upon themselves,
> But they are unjust and foolish.
> *Surah 33:72*

And now let me check the time: oops, so late again!

All right, time for me to learn from experience, just like the human beings of the Bible and the Quran: instead of trying to write just a little bit more, as I usually do, this time I'll go in the kitchen and start making your lunch; otherwise, I can hardly expect you to listen to me again tomorrow. And after lunch, I'll give you an example of someone who has looked at Islam from outside. All Germans know him, and I've already mentioned him several times. Can you guess who it is?

Extra Afternoon Section on Johann Wolfgang von Goethe!

You guessed right: I could hardly name anyone who has more deeply grasped and memorably described the essence of Islam than the German national poet. It's just a shame that so few Germans know what an expert on Islam they have on their own bookshelves. Goethe was already fairly old when he began reading everything about the Middle East that was available in his day. He even learned Arabic so that he could pronounce the Quran with his own lips. And the great thing about his example is: studying a different literature, one that was completely foreign, exotic, in Germany in those days, led him in turn to write the most wondrous poems in his old age, and to add a sequel, the fantastic second part, to his *Faust*. The liberation from familiar patterns of literature is tangible everywhere in his late work: he tried out new forms; he created ingenious German adaptations of the rhythms, motifs and words that he found in the Quran and in Persian poetry.

Much of it shows no outward trace of Middle Eastern culture. The 'Marienbad Elegy', for example, in which Goethe dares to imitate the Sufis' strange audacity of surrendering completely to longing, is simply one of the most beautiful love poems ever written in the German language – and this one by a 74-year-old, a very old man for that time, who had just been rejected in his suit for the hand of a 19-year-old girl. Goethe was ridiculed for that at the time; today he is loved not least for this poem.

The influence of Middle Eastern poetry is most clearly visible in his *West-Eastern Divan*, though. When Goethe published that collection, some said he had secretly converted to Islam. That's nonsense, of course: you don't have to belong to a religion to understand it. You only have to assimilate it, and you can do that thanks to your cognitive faculties, one of which is your imagination. All Goethe himself said about it was: 'All of us live and die in Islam.' By that he meant not the religion founded by the Prophet Muhammad, but the literal sense of *islām* as he understood it – namely, 'submission to God's will'. In this general sense, in the sense that every person is born with a natural or infantile religiousness, or submissiveness to God, Goethe felt himself to be a Muslim too. Converting to

Islam, however, probably never entered his mind for a second; on the contrary: through his enthusiasm for a different, foreign religion, he found his way, in his old age, back to his own religion, Protestant Christianity. And that would be the best effect I could imagine when a Christian, a Jew, a Buddhist or anyone else reads our book: for them to think of their own religion, because everything we're talking about is present in it too in one way or another, in their own language, with their familiar images, with other accents, and with rituals, songs and prayers that don't become ingrained so easily once you're grown up.

To finish this chapter, I'd like to read just one of Goethe's poems with you, in which you'll recognize many themes. It's called 'Talismans', and it begins like this:

Gottes ist der Orient!	To God belongs the Orient!
Gottes ist der Okzident!	To God belongs the Occident!
Nord- und südliches	Northern too and southern
Gelände	lands
Ruht im Frieden seiner Hände.	All rest in His peaceful hands.

Does that ring any bells?

Right, 'To God belongs the Orient! / To God belongs the Occident!' is taken word for word from Surah 2:115, which you have heard. Goethe broadens this geographical indication with 'northern' and 'southern lands' to make it unmistakable that Orient and Occident are meant to signify the whole world. And he closes this stanza with two motifs that we have also seen before: peace, from which the word 'Islam' is derived; and hands, which are the Quran's metaphor for God's power and creative force.

Let's listen to the second Talisman:

Er, der einzige Gerechte	He Who alone is ever Just
Will für jedermann das	Wills every man have what he
Rechte.	must.

Sey, von seinen hundert Namen,	Of all His hundred names this one
Dieser hochgelobet! Amen.	Be highly praised! His will be done.

I assume you know about the ninety-nine names of God. Goethe makes them a hundred because 'ninety-nine names' would be too long for the line – form is essential! – and in fact what is significant isn't any specific number, but the fact that God has infinitely many qualities. And of these names of God, about which Muslim scholars have debated and disputed since the very beginning – Which one is the most significant? Which ones are not so important? – Goethe chooses one: 'the Just'. In doing so, he consciously follows those schools of Islam that declare justice to be the third of the five principles of faith, right after unity and prophethood. I explained about the principles of faith, the *uṣūl*, in the third chapter.

The third Talisman goes like this:

Mich verwirren will das Irren;	Though errancy works to confuse me
Doch du weißt mich zu entwirren.	Thou knowest how to disabuse me.
Wenn ich handle, wenn ich dichte,	In what I do, in what I write,
Gib du meinem Weg die Richte.	Direct me and guide my feet right.

Here Goethe alludes to the Fatiha, the opening surah of the Quran, which is about the hope of not going astray among the many possible paths: that is, not going astray in the freedom that human beings have as vice-regents of God. And Goethe explicitly connects this hope to his own life, his own work: 'In what I do, in what I write'. Goethe was obsessed every time he began studying something, and he tried his hand at all kinds of things, from medicine to the theory of colours to politics, from theology to history to many foreign literatures ('. . . in China if need be!'), from poetry, novels and drama to scientific treatises to autobiography. This stanza hits the exact sense of the word *dalāl*, 'errancy', as it is used in the Quran: namely, as wandering about with no destination or plan, as if you had lost your sense of direction in the desert. The right direction, on the other hand, Goethe's *Richte*, is a literal translation of the word *shari'a*. In the Quran, the word means not 'law', as in today's Arabic, but 'path of divine guidance'.

Now, on to the fourth Talisman:

Ob ich Ird'sches denk' und sinne	Though I ponder on earthly things
Das gereicht zu höherem Gewinne.	The profit is sublime that such thought brings.
Mit dem Staube nicht der Geist zerstoben	Spirit, with terrestrial dust not covered,
Dringet, in sich selbst gedrängt, nach oben.	Rushes, in itself inspired, upward.

The first two lines – 'Though I ponder on earthly things / The profit is sublime that such thought brings' – indicate that everything said in mystical poetry has a double meaning. Love, for example, is love between two people, and at the same time love for God; wine is the earthly drink, and at the same time a heavenly elixir; father and mother mean the speaker's parents, and at the same time the Creator, and so on: everything on earth, even a spittoon, is a name of God, 'so that the Creator is praised with every name that belongs to Him in Creation'.

Who said that, again?

Right, that was the 'Greatest Master', *al-shaykh al-akbar* Ibn Arabi.

The spirit that rushes upward, pressed into itself, in the third and fourth lines, connects the religious notion of the resurrection of the spirit with the physical doctrine that the world consists of tiny particles which dissolve with every death to reconnect again. Goethe thus connects religion and science, and it is this connection that he found especially interesting in Islam.

Finally, the last and longest Talisman, in which there is probably nothing more for me to explain, since you will immediately think of the 'breath of the Merciful' that flows into you every time you take a breath. Just remember how you paid attention to your breathing in and out, and that all of life consists of opposites: birth and death, love and hate, hope and fear, oppression and redemption; only their unity makes them wondrous. You can repeat it after me, because there is no more beautiful prayer for Muslims whose language is German than this one – by a poet who wasn't a Muslim.

Im Atemholen sind zweierlei Gnaden:	In drawing breath are graces twain:
Die Luft einziehn, sich ihrer entladen.	Inhaling air, discharging it again.
Jenes bedrängt, dieses erfrischt;	The former constraining, the latter relieving;
So wunderbar ist das Leben gemischt.	Such a wondrous mixture is living.
Du Danke Gott, wenn er dich preßt,	Thank thou God when He presses thee,
Und dank' ihm, wenn er dich wieder entläßt.	And thank Him when He releases thee.

Reblochon, Pecorino and Appenzeller

D
o you know what occurred to me yesterday after we talked again about the imagination, which is part of the cognitive faculty?

Oh God, another one of my rhetorical questions! One more and I'll owe you a spaghetti sundae.

Anyway, I thought of another reason why the Quran calls Muhammad the 'Seal of the Prophets'. The title could be a clue that human beings, with increasing urbanization, scientific progress and all their technical developments, no longer use their imagination as much as they used to in the desert or in the countryside, where there was nothing round about to distract the senses. After all, you dream better alone in your room at night, and not in the middle of a busy street. With urbanization, the imagination gradually atrophied, like a muscle that doesn't get exercised any more, so that no one else had a prophetic gift after Muhammad. Something of the prophetic imagination has been preserved only in poets such as Goethe, or mystics such as Ibn Arabi – otherwise they wouldn't have been able to put themselves in other people's place, nor would they have travelled in their imaginations up to Heaven.

How do you like my theory? Persuasive? Ingenious? Ground-breaking?

Okay, okay – I didn't want to know in such detail.

Sudden End of the Ingenious Ground-breaking Theory!

So we have God, we have human beings, and we have a relationship between the two. What does this relationship consist of? Like any other relationship, it consists mainly of communication. God speaks, and human beings answer. Even turning away is an answer; even denying God is a reaction, a 'No' to questions that human beings ask themselves on their deathbed, if not before. And human beings speak too, in prayers and songs, praise and lamentation, looks and actions, and sometimes they hear the answer, and sometimes they don't.

God speaks. When I say that, you'll think first of the scriptures: the Bible, the Quran, perhaps also the Vedas, the Tao Te Ching and so on. A revelation is a form of communication, of course, and I have said often enough that what God sends down to people is poetry, not an instruction booklet. But today I would like to discuss a communication that is much more fundamental. What can you do to communicate without words – let's say, if you're thirsty, or if you want to tell someone where there's a buried treasure? Right: you make signs.

> And among His signs is that from you He created mates
> That you may rest with them,
> And compassion and love between you.
> Behold, therein are signs for those who reflect.
> And among His signs is the creation of the Heavens and the
>   Earth
> And the diversity of your languages and your colours.
> Behold, therein are signs for those who know.

And among His signs is your sleep at night, or during the day,
And your quest for His bounty.
Behold, therein are signs for those who hear.
And among His signs is the lightning
Which you watch in fear or hope,
And the fact that He sends down water from the sky,
With which He revives the Earth after its death.
Behold, therein are signs for those who are wise.
And among His signs is the fact that Heaven and Earth stand
    still at His command;
Then, when He calls you out of the Earth, lo, you rise up to
    Heaven.
And to Him belong all in the Heavens and the Earth;
All obey Him.
And it is He who brings forth Creation,
Then He repeats it, which is easy for Him.
And His likeness is supreme in the Heavens and the Earth;
He is the Mighty, the Wise.

Surah 30:21ff.

The Quran, like the Bible, teaches that everything in the world, and everything that happens in the world, including our neighbour Norbert and his incessantly yapping beagle, and even the beagle's mess that I step in, contains a message from God to human beings (bearing in mind His warped sense of humour, perhaps). The Quran itself calls this an allegory that is in the heavens and on earth. 'Allegory' is a poetic form of expression, as when you communicate an idea by an image. I'll give you an example: 'The river that springs forth from its source and flows down to the sea' could be an image for the course of a person's lifetime.

I admit my example is something you might find in a greetings card or in your friendship album, if you still had one.

The Quran's allegories are more unusual, surprising, mysterious, and that was a source of fascination to Muhammad's

listeners, even in the beginning. Even a fly, says the Quran
– God can make even a fly into an allegory of human beings.
In other words, He speaks to us through nature. And not
only through nature, but also through the diversity of peoples
and languages, through sleep and waking, day and night. 'I
was a treasure and wanted to be known,' says God according
to a *ḥadīth qudsī*, a saying of the Prophet, 'therefore I created the world.' Nothing that exists stands simply for itself.
Everything – nature as well as civilization, art, love, food,
history, the twittering of the birds, human kindness and,
not least, sexuality – all things in the world are at the same
time 'signs', we are told everywhere in the Quran. In Arabic:
'āyāt.

But do you know what the verses of the Quran themselves
are called?

Okay, okay, you get a spaghetti sundae.

Quran verses are also called *'āyāt*, 'signs'. We could also say,
conversely, that Creation is all one big poem that God sings
to human beings. *Khalq*, the Arabic word for 'creation', also
means, not coincidentally, 'form, model, shape', in the sense
that a sculptor or a potter forms, models, shapes the stone or
the clay. And the result is more than just functional – it is also
beautiful.

And the beasts He created:
In them you have clothing, labour, food;
But in your eyes they also have beauty
When you drive them in at night and out in the morning.
And they carry your burdens to countries
Otherwise unreachable without tribulations of the soul.
Behold, your Lord is kind and merciful.
And He created the horses, the camels, the asses
For you to ride upon
But also as ornament.

Surah 16:5ff.

Let's suppose you were to ask me even more questions than you have up to now – endless questions for that matter, such as, let's say, Why is there the chestnut tree outside our window? Why was there the chestnut that the chestnut tree outside our window grew from? Why was there the bird that dropped the chestnut on the ground from which the chestnut tree grew outside our window? Why were there the bird's parents who . . . and so on and so on: the reason for the reason for the reason for the reason . . . where would you end up then?

Right: at the Big Bang.

And now remember the Creation story in the Bible and in the Quran. There too, everything follows organically from a single original beginning – God's first word – so that human beings, if they just keep looking and searching further, can always find an empirical, verifiable reason for all the manifestations of life: from the light of the sun to the formation of water to the earth, the plants, the animals, the human beings. That is, in contrast to the ethnic religions or the ancient Chinese and Indian worldviews, heaven is not full of spirits and mythical beings that have their own free will and are therefore unpredictable. In Judaism, Christianity and Islam, stars, the sun, the moon and water have no independent power. No, they too are signs of God, and thus part of a cosmic plan: 'And to Him belong all in the Heavens and the Earth', says Surah 30, which we were reading just now; 'All obey Him.'

But not only that: everything that exists is always explainable by reliable mechanisms of causation; every cell in your body can be traced back, theoretically, to the very beginning of Creation. As the physicists have discovered, the whole universe is subject to the same laws: the black holes the same as the solar flares and the Northern Lights on earth. But that also means everything is connected to everything by an endless braid of cause and effect. The fact that there seems to be so much chaos today, humanity running amok and nature in peril – who knows? Maybe it has to do with the fact that this is still the seventh day, God's day of rest after having created human beings.

Certainly, in our day-to-day experience, life often seems random, arbitrary; we see no reason why someone should die young, a tsunami should wash tens of thousands of innocent people to their death, or a star should burn out in the sky. Believing in God means perceiving order nevertheless, behind all the random events, contradictions and even the injustices: an order that embraces the whole universe. It means exploring, experiencing, describing the universe as something 'formed, moulded, shaped': as a celestial work of art, if you like. When I look inside myself during prayer, or concentrate specifically on my breathing, I sometimes experience God even within myself. Reading the signs that He incessantly shows us, being in harmony with yourself and enjoying Creation is worshipping God in Islam.

Wait a minute, you may think now – enjoyment is supposed to be worshipping God? Yes, if you take to heart God's word that He created the world in order to make Himself known, then you serve God when you appreciate this world: when you look not just for its utility, but also admire its 'ornaments' (as they're called in Surah 16), when you enjoy life – and when you clean up your room, by the way. Because Islam doesn't make the distinction Christianity does between the sacred and the profane, between the heavenly and the earthly. That's why Muslims, when they begin a speech, so often say – and why the inscription over the door of Grandpa and Grandma's house in Spain says – *bismillah*, 'In the name of God'. And when they hope for something, they murmur *inshallah*: 'God willing'. And when something wondrous happens, they cry *mashallah!* 'What God has willed!' And when they are content, they sigh *alhamdulillah* – 'Praise be to God!' Everything on earth, even the most mundane chores, are worship; even the most unprepossessing objects are a gift of God. So that includes your room!

Think sometime about whether it is really worthy of your rank and your responsibility as a caliphess of God that you drop absolutely everything on the floor – jackets, books, chess pieces, papers, wrappers, pens, even socks and underwear, dirty ones no less. It's my room, you answer me every time I scold you; it's none of your business. No, I'm telling you, it's a part of the world; treat it respectfully, make the place you're responsible for beautiful – and, most of all, throw the rubbish out!

God is beautiful and loves beauty.

Hadith

I admit this hadith, this saying of the Prophet, doesn't refer directly to children's rooms, which didn't exist yet in those days in Mecca.

Heavens, yes! Even the Quran occasionally digresses and inserts a few extra lines from the Meccans' day-to-day life among all the sublime ideas. It answers a mother's question how long she should breastfeed her child, for example, or rants about a neighbour who is even more annoying than our Norbert. We would be trivializing the scriptures if we were to take such topical information and exclamations as their ever-lasting message. After all, I don't always find all neighbours stupid just because I'm occasionally annoyed at Norbert. And the Quran likewise always refers to specific persons when it rants from time to time about Jews or Christians, and often enough about the Muslims themselves. But you should clean up your room all the same! After all, 'topical' means concerned with the here and now.

But to get back to the Prophet: it was his custom to go out-side with his torso bare whenever it rained, and he said the rain came fresh from his Lord. 'Is there anything more full of light, more sublime and clear?' asks Ibn Arabi, in whose works I read this tradition. 'Thus the rain enchanted the noblest of people by its closeness to his Lord; the rain was like the heavenly messenger who brought him the divine revelation.'

Now, rain on the Arabian peninsula was something special – definitely not an everyday event. So it's not a very good example. I'll try another way: You are soon going to reach the age when, although you'll find it annoying at first, your body will change, and with it your needs, interests and opinions. It was my great fortune, I know today, that my parents were completely relaxed about such matters. They taught me that love, including physical love, tenderness, desire, is a beautiful thing, and not something dirty. That it was nothing to be ashamed of when I had my first ejaculation. And so we will always communicate to you too, I hope, that sexuality is a gift, one that can bring an infinite amount of joy, but also one that you should handle with care.

That's not convincing either?

All right, I realize even as I'm writing that you're going to raise your eyebrows at this: Papa, don't talk like that; it's embarrassing.

Well, then, think of a situation you remember yourself: think of your grandpa when he looked at the sea from his terrace in Spain, or when he ate a delicious piece of watermelon. And think of how proud he was of his grandchildren, how his heart rejoiced in you – in those moments, your grandpa always said, or murmured, *Khodāyā!* – that is, more or less, 'My God!'

When I was a child, I thought that was just a figure of speech, until I realized: no, he means it quite seriously. He's really speaking to God in such moments. He's happy on the terrace in Spain in summer with the delicious watermelon, or at home in Cologne when I buy him a good cheese. Yes, cheese! Your grandma only ever bought the pre-sliced yellow plastic from Aldi, which your grandpa was not ecstatic about. And so when I brought your grandpa a really good French, Italian or Swiss cheese, then when he cut a little wedge of it and looked at it, felt its consistency, and finally put it in his mouth, in that moment it was like a little revelation. I won't go so far as to say he absorbed God, but in the complex aromas he tasted more than just the Reblochon, the pecorino or the Appenzeller on his tongue: he tasted the preciousness of the world. In other words, by just a bit of cheese – very good cheese, of course, not sliced plastic – he felt himself connected with all of Creation, and thus with its – his – Creator. And he murmured, *Khodāyā!*

And now, my dear daughter, now I can give you the simplest and best and most memorable explanation – I'm going to patent it – of what a saint is. A saint is someone who would cry out in rapture even at Grandma's flavour-free pre-sliced plastic cheese from Aldi: *Khodāyā!* In other words, someone who sees God in everything, even in trivial things, even in the mosquito that bites them; even in a spittoon, whether big or little; even in their misfortune, in their distress:

> But give good tidings to those who are patient!
> Who say, when calamity befalls them, 'We belong to God,
> And to Him we return.'
> It is they who receive the blessings
> Of their Lord, and mercy,
> And they who are rightly guided.
>   *Surah* 2:155f.

You've noticed by now that I'm obsessed with language – it reveals so much! Here's another example: the Quran calls 'unbelief' *kufr*. But guess what the Arabic word *kufr* means literally.

Well?

Kufr means 'ingratitude' – that is, when you receive something as a gift and still complain about it. In the Quran, an unbeliever is someone who doesn't value their own life, and all life; remember Goethe's last 'Talisman': 'Thank thou God when He presses thee, / And thank Him when He releases thee.'

Conversely, faith is not an attitude or a belief, it's a response: gratitude.

God brought you forth
From your mothers' wombs;
You knew nothing then.
And He gave you hearing, eyes, hearts;
Maybe you are grateful.
Surah 16:78

A person who is not a Muslim, who doesn't even use the word God perhaps, but is grateful for life and appreciates it, protects it, enjoys and respects it, is to me a more devout person than one who trumpets out the profession of faith while destroying the world, or while wanting to own more and more, more wealth, more power, more fame. And the wonderful thing is that not only human beings can be faithful, but God too:

Whoso does good voluntarily,
Behold, God is grateful and knowing.
Surah 2:158

Communication between God and His creatures is not a monologue, it's a conversation. You could almost say that, just as God made man and woman out of the one person, He made the person out of Himself, to rest with Him in love and compassion. By this logic, God would need people in order to be God, just as it is the existence of the woman that makes the man a man, and vice versa.

Now your grandpa, as I said, was not a saint, and in younger years he was nowhere near it. He would complain, asking why Grandma had bought those cheese slices that taste like nothing again, and the row would begin. Because your grandma called your grandpa ungrateful (faithless, so to speak!), and said he should do the shopping himself. As if she had time to hunt up some delicatessen; did he have any idea how much she had to carry; didn't someone in the household have to keep an eye on expenses; and so on and so forth, all in her shrill voice, until your grandpa finally grumbled that he hadn't asked for anything but a simple cheese with a little flavour – why did she always disregard his needs and always buy what she liked, not what he liked? My God, Grandma moaned then, *Khodāyā!* She bought the wrong cheese one time and he's freaking out. And you know what happens when someone you're angry with tells you not to freak out: then you really freak out. And sure enough, your grandpa roared in his thundering voice that made the neighbours jump out of their socks, and God no doubt groaned once more:

No one is as quarrelsome as human beings!
                     Surah 18:54

At least now you understand why I was your grandpa's favourite, since I was the one who brought him Reblochon, pecorino and Appenzeller all at once. You could almost say, if the cheese was a gift of God, then I was the messenger. So have a little more respect!

Oh, I'm exaggerating again, am I? I always exaggerate when I start telling stories? My God – *khodāyā!* – that happens to be my job as a writer. If I always told it exactly the way it happened, my books would be as boring to read as the minutes of a meeting, and then no one would buy them, and you wouldn't get any allowance. So just be grateful (faithful!) for once that God has endowed us with an imagination, with creativity. God Himself embellishes His stories with whatever occurs to Him – otherwise they'd be theology. And the best stories –Surah 12, verse 3, remember! – are still those that He tells.

However, I'll admit your grandma and grandpa didn't really have a row over a bit of cheese, or at least not such a loud one. I only wanted to show you how conflicts arise – in our kitchen when I was a boy and in the world generally. And that is, when you get to the bottom of it, by people feeling misunderstood or unappreciated. In other words, not seen. And the same thing goes, oddly enough, for our relationship to God. God wants to be seen, for whatever reason. He could just as well have created everything and then leaned back and enjoyed it in silence, say, or just been content to watch. Some of the earlier religions taught exactly that: God created the world and then He leaned back, so to speak. The God of the Bible and the Quran, however, kept making signs to the people, and because many of them didn't look, He sent all the prophets, to every nation in their own language, to make Himself understood. That's how it is when you love someone: you want to be loved back, and perhaps that is the whole problem. That we human beings want something in return for our love. If nothing else, then at least gratitude.

That's probably why the stories in the Bible, in the Quran, in all the other scriptures and also in humanity's great myths – from the Indian Gilgamesh epic to the Persian Book of Kings or the Iliad – are so human, with jealousy, flattery, threats, desire, courting, doubt, deceit, spite, violence and even hatred, which is so often the opposite face of love. Yes, those are dramas: great, passionate, sometimes brutal dramas; love dramas, you might say, between God and human beings, between Creation as a whole – nature, fate, life, endlessness – and the individual creature. But peace – no, peace doesn't come only in Paradise. There was peace every time your grandma and grandpa embraced each other once more. Or when I put the right cheese on the table. Even Grandma had a bit.

The Centre of the Universe

Yesterday you said you understood the part about the cheese, and even about the spittoon, but Norbert's beagle's messes are simply disgusting.

I suppose you're right. When I stepped in one, I didn't shout *Khodāyā!* What a wonderful sign from God! I just said . . . oh, you know. I'm your grandpa's son, after all! Now imagine that had happened to Jesus: instead of freaking out like me, he probably would have maintained his serenity and his friendly demeanour, and that, when you think about it, would have been the far better and healthier reaction, for himself as well as others. And, besides, imagine Norbert: how surprised he would be, and how ashamed, if someone remained friendly even right after stepping in a mess. Norbert would be much more likely to apologize for his beagle than if he got yelled at, as I yell at him, and maybe he'd even remember to take his little bag the next time they go walkies. Jesus' 'turn the other cheek' was meant politically, and wasn't simply naive at all, as I myself described it a few days ago.

Fend off the evil with the good,
And see, your enemy becomes a close friend.

Surah 41:34

This example allows me to explain better what I meant the day before yesterday when I talked about the difference between self-perfection and self-fulfilment. Self-fulfilment means: I let it all hang out. Self-perfection, on the other hand, means: I don't get worked up about every little thing. And perfection means more still than just keeping cool. When Jesus and his disciples came across a half-decomposed dead dog with its muzzle hanging open, the disciples muttered in disgust, 'What an awful stench!' But Jesus cried out, happy as a child, 'Look how brilliantly white its teeth shine!'

This and countless other stories about Jesus, by the way, are not found in the Gospel; they are stories the Sufis told, and that may go to show you once again that no prophet belongs to just one particular religion. Here you encounter an Islamic Jesus, and by the same token Goethe shows you a Christian Muhammad; in contemporary American authors, for example, you can find a Jewish interpretation of Buddha – and it is precisely these intersections, cross-references and appropriations that make the religions so much more attractive, rich, and also more conciliatory than if each one could only fit in one pigeonhole. Because the intersections, cross-references and appropriations don't make everything the same. No, they add to the peculiarities, and perhaps lend a new sense to the Prophet's saying that you already know: 'The paths to God are as numerous as the breaths a person takes.'

To return once more to communication: God speaks to us not only through love, the sea or cheese. He also speaks in words: in Hebrew, Arabic, Chinese, ancient Persian; probably in all the languages of India; or, if you believe what the Quran says, in every language to every people. These are revelations in the strict sense: verbal communications from God, whether or not they are recorded in the form of books.

What the revelations say about God varies greatly, of course, depending first of all on whether they tell of just one God or many gods. The messages themselves are likewise diverse: one revelation emphasizes love; another, hope for the next life; and Islam, again and again, the equality between people which follows from the unity of God.

A Brief Supplement about Equality!

The Prophet's message that no person is above another was actually revolutionary for his time, and that is why his message electrified mainly the slaves, the disadvantaged, the disenfranchised, the orphans and also the women in Mecca: neither the rich are above the poor nor the light-skinned above the dark; neither the natives above the foreigners nor one tribe above another; and in particular – if you read the whole Quran attentively and study its language, instead of picking out individual verses – one sex is not above the other. On the pilgrimage, Muslims have always experienced that equality: no matter where they come from and no matter how old or aristocratic they are, all of them wear the same simple white garment, just a seamless cloth to be exact. Later, Muslims are buried in that same cloth, so that they are all equal in death too.

Now, I have not yet made the pilgrimage, and to be honest I am a little apprehensive about it, because Mecca today with its glitzy shopping malls hardly seems spiritual. And with its underpaid, practically disenfranchised migrant workers from Pakistan and Bangladesh, it can hardly be a place where equality reigns either. It's not much better in Iran, where they had a revolution in 1979 in the name of the disadvantaged and the downtrodden – an Islamic revolution, no less – and today the gap between rich and poor is bigger than ever.

When I want to remember how much Islam emphasizes human equality, I visit the beautiful old mosques: there, in the prayer courtyard, there is a pit, from a few centimetres to as much as a metre deep, into which the imam leading the prayers has to descend, so that the leader of the congregation is lower than the other worshippers. Look for that the next time we're in Isfahan. In the big mosques there are two pits, in fact: one for the male and one for the female prayer leader, and men and women shared the courtyard with equal space. It was a long time ago that it was really that equal, if ever – but you understand the principle; you can step down into the prayer leader's pit and think about why the reality has turned out different.

End of the Extra Section on Equality!

At the same time, though, the revelations have a great deal in common: they advocate good works, humility and compassion, for example. But, most of all, they set a short human life span in relation to the eternity of death. They also set human beings, whose view of the world is limited to what they can see through their own eyes, in relation to the whole universe. Ultimately, all revelations create a cosmic order, assigning the individual creature a place in Creation.

God, who raised up the Heavens
With no pillars that you can see,
Then took His seat on the throne
And bent Sun and Moon to His service,
Each orbit in its predetermined interval.
He directs all things
And reveals the signs;
Maybe you will believe in the meeting with your Lord.
It is He who has spread out the Earth,
Set mountains upon it, laid rivers in it,
And made in it of every fruit a pair.
He makes night cover up the day.
Behold, therein are signs for those who reflect.

Surah 13:2ff.

That is the core of every religion: to recognize in Creation, and in every single breath, an order, something formed, willed, good, meaningful, even if the meaning isn't always knowable. In other words: to deny that life is just a senseless fluke. But that is also the purpose of every religion, because otherwise human beings would feel lost the minute they looked up into the starry sky. And how much more so when they look their own death in the eye.

> And not for nothing have we created
> Heaven and Earth
> And what is between them.
> ### Surah 38:27

I read in an old book a funny, somehow disturbing calculation: imagine the entire history of the Earth from the beginning to today was shrunk down until it fit into just one year. It would have taken from 1 January until the end of April before life came into existence, and then it would have taken until September for the first single-celled algae to evolve. In early October, the first protozoans, also single-cell organisms, paddled around in the ocean; in mid-October, hurrah! the multi-cellular animals arrive, although only invertebrates. By the end of November, fish-like vertebrates finally venture onto land; in early December, amphibians are wriggling about on the beach, and soon afterwards, Earth greets the first reptiles.

Now things speed up!

Towards the end of December, little mouselike mammals appear, and on New Year's Eve the great apes divide from the main trunk of the primates. At about 9:12 in the evening, some early hominids can be discerned, which continue to evolve until our ancestors walk upright, discover fire, and gradually become sedentary. Everything we call history – that is, the last 6,000 years, the period we more or less have records of – happens in the last 39 seconds of the year. Or in a much

shorter time, to be more accurate, because scientists now esti-
mate the age of the Earth to be not 4 to 5 billion years, as that
book had it, but closer to 20 billion years. So the human period
in comparison to the history of our planet has shrunk to little
more than ten seconds out of a year.

Ten seconds for the entire history of humanity! And the
history of the Earth in turn would probably be just a year out
of thousands and millions of years if you include other solar
systems that are much older than our planet. That makes you
realize how insignificant an individual life is, and even the
life of a clan or a nation; how fleeting our languages are, our
civilization, our ideals – to say nothing of our feelings and
everything we do. It is hard to attribute even the least importance to our own fate when you have an inkling of the size and
age of the universe.

But if our existence is so insignificant, a person might just as
well do whatever they felt like: murder, theft, cruelty whenever
the opportunity arose. What difference would it make to the
universe what a person ... no, what the human race does?
Who would even care if one of them kills another? Seen from
another star, even a nuclear war would be nothing more than
a brief flicker in the telescope – it might even be pretty to see.

You could also make a similar calculation with distances:
if our galaxy, the Milky Way, were shrunk to the size of the
Earth, then our whole solar system with all its planets wouldn't
even be as big as a grain of sand. And on that scale, which probably isn't up to date any more, the next grain of sand – that is,
the next solar system – would be about 100 kilometres away.
A hundred kilometres of empty space between two grains of
sand, and our Earth is no bigger than a speck of dust on one
of them! And those are the dimensions just within our own
Milky Way, which is only one of countless galaxies. It beg-
gars reason to think that what happens on our tiny, fragile
Earth, and whether I am a good or a bad person, could have
any importance at all. And yet the Quran says, and all the

revelations say, exactly that: yes, it has importance; not just the Earth, but every single life.

Whoever saves one person's life, it shall be
As if he had saved all humanity.

Surah 5:32

But the pinnacle of Creation? Yes, the pinnacle of Creation: God has brought forth this universe just for us. That sounds mad, and yet there lies a deep, naturally paradoxical truth in it: in order for human beings to do more than just grow and decay again like vegetables – to experience the world as conscious beings and have a sense of what is proper and what is wrong – they have to believe in their own importance. And they have to lose that belief again. Let me try to illustrate what I mean using your own consciousness.

A baby is born and doesn't know what 'I' means. Even when it starts to learn how to talk, it usually speaks of itself in the third person. Let's say the baby's name is Anne: she doesn't say, 'I eat too' or 'Me ouch'; in the beginning she says, 'Anne eat too', 'Anne ouch'. The baby doesn't yet know herself as something separate and special, something distinct from all the other people who come into her perception. That's why it's critical for her future life that the baby's parents show her from the beginning: You're important to me! Because a person who is loved understands that she is lovable, and gradually the 'You're important *to me*' in the child's consciousness develops into 'You are important!'

When the child says 'I' for the first time, at the age of 2, 3 years, that's not only a grammatical breakthrough. It's the realization in her mind: I'm an 'I'! The child no longer simply has sensations and desires: she now knows they are her own sensations and desires that belong only to her. She discovers that she is different from the other yous, shes, hes and theys around her. This peculiar word 'I' is reserved only for herself.

From there, from her I, the child looks out upon the whole world. Discovering self-awareness means a tremendous elevation of oneself – which corresponds to the elevation of human beings over all other creatures in the Creation story. Humanity too, because it feels itself loved by God, feels itself to be the centre of the universe: We are important!

Soon, however, the child discovers that all the other people around her also say 'I'. That means she now has to become sure of herself – in a twofold sense: sure of herself in the sense of 'self-assured', and also in the sense of 'sure that she is' – in order to realize that the world has many centres, so to speak, and all the other I's feel themselves no less important. Thus, the child gradually learns to relativize her own importance, to see herself as just one of many I's, until, one day, usually during the transition to adulthood, on looking up into the starry sky, or down at her parents' grave, or when her beloved leaves her, she realizes how perfectly insignificant she is. Very many cases of mental illness involve a narcissistic personality disorder, or exaggerated self-importance: the person's I is no longer able to relativize its importance adequately. The cause of the disorder, however, is often that the person has not felt appreciated enough. The excessive egocentrism is a reaction, so to speak. This is true of individuals, but it can also be applied to societies – and maybe to our contemporary Western society.

In the same way, humanity as a whole needs first to feel uniquely loved by and important to God. Because only then can the human race realize that all the other living creatures on this planet – and all other planets – grew up believing, so to speak, that the universe was created just for them. A philosopher once put it very pointedly with the question: How would a horse answer the question what God is like? It would say, Like a horse, what else? Unlike horses, however, human beings are able to realize that the world doesn't just revolve around them – it revolves around every other creature too. According to human beings, anyway.

Because, if you are devout, such a diminished importance is not a flaw, nor is it a cause for regret. On the contrary, not thinking themselves so important is the necessary precondition for human beings to approach godliness, surpassing even their initial elevation as caliphs of God: the human race loses its uniqueness, which is only appearance, and sees itself as one with all creatures, with the whole universe. In other words, precisely by no longer wanting anything for themselves, and not even thinking of their elementary needs (to the point that some mystics even forget to eat and drink, or no longer feel pain) – by the annihilation of their I, human beings rise above – transcend – their self. To resort again to the image of a river – which is not so stupid really, although somewhat worn for having served in so much verse and in so many poetry albums – the soul, after coming forth from a single spring, flows into the ocean into which all springs flow. That is the teaching of the Upanishads, the ancient Indian books, and of all mystical religions, including Islamic mysticism. But it is also what happens, I believe, to every person when they die.

When they die?

When a person dies, in Islam and probably in almost all religions, the soul leaves the body and, in a moment of transition, the person sees themselves from above, their body with its heart no longer beating, their loved ones around them, until their consciousness finally dissolves or joins with what the Hindus call the world soul, *atman*. That is why, on Grandpa's grave and on that of every Muslim, it says, 'We belong to God, and to Him we return.' Aziz Nasafi, a Sufi who lived around the same time as Ibn Arabi, describes it this way:

> On every creature's death, the spirit returns to the spiritual world and the body to the physical world. But only the body changes. The spiritual world is a single spirit behind the physical world, which shines through every single being that comes into existence like a light shining through a window. Depending on

the kind and the size of the window, less light or more shines into the world. But the light itself is unchanging.

Is that how it is? We will only find out, of course, when we die ourselves. But believing it took away your grandpa's fear of death, and the belief also gives me hope that our few years on earth are only a transition, a barely perceptible fraction of those 10 seconds that all humanity has lasted so far. Afterwards, life will go on in some other way, although I will probably no longer think 'I'. I didn't think it in my mother's belly either, and everything was fine there, I assume.

'*Khodāyā*,' Rumi cried, 'when You take my life, death is sweet as sugar.' Your grandpa smiled as he waved good-bye to us. And yet I wept.

life Itself

I often think: the Quran, the Bible, the Tao Te Ching, all of humanity's holy books – they're not visions, doctrines or philosophies; they aren't anything invented or imagined. They are experiences that are remembered in the form of images, stories, rituals because they are too intricate for reason, too disturbing for ordinary lessons, too paradoxical for a dissertation: they are the experiences of peoples and the experiences of individuals; the experience of cold and heat, spring and autumn, drought and harvest; and also of war and peace, injustice and redemption; not least, the experience of being in love, of hate, jealousy, reconciliation. The holy scriptures are also buried memories of the months in our mother's womb and finally our birth itself, which is presumably still more painful for the baby than for the mother, and certainly more frightening. They are experiences of humanity which have taken the form of verses in the minds of certain individuals, and we call those individuals prophets.

Just think: life probably begins – almost every life – in mortal panic as the baby is pressed by an unknown, overwhelming and undetermined power through the narrow birth canal. Where the first chapter of Genesis says, 'And there was light', that

is not just a poetic allegory; it is very concretely the first –
and perhaps the deeply disturbing – impression of a human
being coming into the world. Yes, religion is the comfort of
the baby's first cuddle; it is the contentment of sucking at the
mother's breast; religion is growing up and bringing up, work
and rest, fragility and care, mortality and grief. Religion is the
guilt feelings and the pain, the trauma and longing that slumber in our subconscious. Paradise, for example – maybe it's
not so very different from our mother's womb: security, cosy
warmth, nutrition in abundance, the delightful juices flowing
through the umbilical cord.

> The likeness of Paradise which has been promised to the
>   godfearing:
> In it are streams of water that does not grow stagnant,
> And streams of milk that never sours,
> And streams of wine delectable to the drinkers,
> And streams of honey unclouded.
> Fruits of every kind are there,
> And forgiveness from their Lord.
>   Surah 47:15

As a child I found it hard to believe in Paradise and Hell. It just
didn't seem realistic to me that there should be a garden in
Heaven where the blessed are spoiled by good-looking service
staff, and a fire deep under the Earth where the damned roast
eternally without burning up. And I didn't understand either
why a God Who is all-merciful should write down our sins
and good deeds as fastidiously as an accountant so that He can
present our bill on Judgement Day. I didn't know yet that the
Quran itself tells of a 'likeness of Paradise', and thus does not
at all imply that it will really be like that.

Later, I heard of the great mystic Rabia, who in the eighth
century walked through Basra, a city in what is now Iraq, carrying a bucket of water in one hand and a torch in the other.

When she was asked what the water and the torch were for, she answered, 'I want to extinguish Hell and burn down Paradise so that God will be loved only for His eternal beauty.'

That made sense to me right away. No one wants to be loved for their money, or for their power, or for their fame. We all want to be loved for our own sake. So it is not a bad question – if I can give you this piece of advice for your future choice of a partner – whether you would be satisfied with your lover in a poor cottage, or if they are weak, disabled, grouchy or a terrible snorer – that is, without all the glitter and shine. God also longs for love that lasts through good times and bad, and He doesn't let us down even when we show our ugliest side. Love is not a contract that rewards obedience and punishes disloyalty. Just as Rabia the saint didn't want anyone to love God out of fear of punishment or out of hope for reward, the Quran too promises something still better than Paradise if you surrender to God with no ulterior goal.

God has promised the believers,
Men and women,
Gardens through which rivers flow,
Forever to dwell therein,
And goodly dwelling-places in the Gardens of Eden.
But God's goodwill is greater than these;
That is the great blessing.

Surah 9:72

And yet humanity has always used the symbolism of punishment and reward, if not in all religions, then in the vast majority of them, to exhort believers to reform and to do good works. That is not just silliness or a teaching method for the intellectually challenged, I think today. It is based, consciously or unconsciously, on the realization that everything we do has consequences, even when they are not visible; that we are accountable even when no one is watching; that doing good is worthwhile even – and especially – when no other person notices it.

> Not the weight of a speck of dust
> On Earth or in Heaven
> Is concealed from thy Lord.
> ### Surah 10:61

To say 'God punishes' is an expression for the awareness of causality, which exists everywhere in the universe. Or would you call nature petty because it's so incredibly exact about cause and effect? Human beings do not have the innocence animals have; we know the difference between good and evil. That means we have responsibility. And what kind of responsibility would that be if misconduct had no consequences, nor good deeds either? And if no one else sees me or thanks me, my comportment still has an effect on the world. God's punishment or reward gives the world a voice inside me.

> Behold, I do not waste
> The work of any labourer among you,
> Whether male or female.
> ### Surah 3:195

At the same time, the knowledge that God is the judge is also a relief, a load off our shoulders: *He* judges so that *we* don't need to judge.

> Judgement is God's alone.
> He tells the truth,
> And He is the best arbiter.
> ### Surah 6:57

If I pursue that thought further – making use of my faculty of reason – I come to the personal conclusion that the death penalty is incompatible with belief in God: no human being has the right to pass a definitive judgement on another. And without arrogating judgement to myself, I can understand how difficult it is for many believers to accept abortions, artificial insemination, genetic engineering, surrogate pregnancy, assisted suicide and so on.

And God gives life and death;
And God sees what you do!
Surah 3:156

You could object that, as it happens, the Quran provides for the death penalty, or point out that the Quran doesn't mention abortion, artificial fertilization, genetic science, surrogate pregnancy or assisted dying at all. So how can I arrive at my conclusions? I arrive at them – and perhaps they are only conjectures – because the same thing is true of the Quran that a famous physicist, Carl Friedrich von Weizsäcker, once said about the Bible: you can either take the Quran seriously, or you can take it literally. You in turn will pursue those thoughts further than I.

Perhaps you've noticed that the Quran says over and over that people who do evil sin against themselves, against their own soul.

If you do good, you do good to yourselves;
And if you do evil, it is to yourselves.
Surah 17:7

That could mean an evil person acts against their own nature, which is originally good and divine. But it could also mean that the punishment is their own consciousness, their own memory, when they die. When I had just got my driving licence, I once spun your uncle's car out of control while I was driving through the woods one winter evening. I remember it as if it was yesterday how, in those one or at most two seconds, while the car slid across the ice as if in slow motion – my whole life passed before my mind's eye in a time lapse film: every happy thing, every sad thing, and all the things I had neglected to do. I saw myself as a child, as an adolescent, as a young adult who, an eternity ago, thought he was a really good driver.

Many people who have survived an accident or thought they were going to die tell the same story or one like it; it's a well-known phenomenon whose causes have not yet been sufficiently studied. In your last moments, you see your whole life go past again on fast-forward. Although 'fast' doesn't really describe the stream of consciousness: actually, you don't have any awareness of time at all. It is as if your existence was concentrated into an infinitesimal point. Not only the universe develops from a tiny cell, but every finite life as well.

I don't know what would have happened next in my mind's eye if the car hadn't come to a stop, by a lucky fluke or by divine providence, right between two tree trunks. I can only say that, since that experience of timelessness, which, as I said, only lasted a second, or two at the most, I have at least an inkling how heavily my faults will weigh. And how deep the satisfaction will be if I manage to perform one good deed or another. How agonizing a smouldering dispute is, and how splendid a reconciliation feels. That was my own Hell, my own Paradise, both at the same time in the same place.

God will forgive us; we can trust in that. He does not keep records like an accountant. God keeps records like a lover who interprets everything to his beloved's advantage.

> Before God created Heaven and Earth, He wrote a note to Himself with His own hand and laid it under His throne. It says, 'My compassion takes precedence over My wrath.'
>
> Hadith

Ibn Arabi and most Sufis believe that eternal damnation would be inconsistent with the infinite mercy that God 'has prescribed for Himself' (Surah 6:54). They consider possible, at most, a Purgatory, a temporary punishment, so that it matters whether you do good or evil, and even this reckoning is interpreted to your advantage.

> Whoever brings a good deed shall have the same tenfold,
> And whoever brings an evil deed shall have but the same.
> And they shall not be wronged.
>
> *Surah 6:160*

As I was skidding towards the woods, it felt like an eternity; objectively it would have only taken one, two seconds before the car smashed into a tree. Thus I may well have had a taste of Purgatory, or a picture of the Last Judgement, as I helplessly turned the steering wheel left and right.

Since then, I understand why the Christians write on a dead person's grave 'Rest in Peace'. And why the Muslims pray for the dead person's soul to rejoice. My uncle, who you never met, 'Mr Engineer' Kermani, went round to all the people to whom he owed something, made peace with all those he had had disagreements with, and gave the poor people he provided for a bonus, before he went to bed one evening and was dead of a heart attack the next morning. No one knows whether he had foreseen that he wouldn't wake up again. But he knew he would have a heavy burden to bear if he took his baggage with him from this world to the next. The Christian Lord's Prayer expresses the same thing, in a way: 'Forgive us our debts, *as we* forgive our debtors.' That means we are supposed to follow the divine example. God will forgive us; we can trust in that. But to rest in peace, we must not leave any strife behind us. Bitterness in this life affects the joy of the next life.

I'm sure you have a thousand objections again where this or that one of my images doesn't add up. A child psychologist would roll their eyes when I call you the successor of God on earth to get you to clean up your room. Your Religious

Education teacher would shake her head because I make Jesus step in dog poo. And my mechanic would say I'm losing my marbles when I use my car accident to explain Heaven and Hell. But maybe it's a little clearer to you now what I mean when I so often point out that the Quran, the Bible, the Vedas, the Tao Te Ching aren't talking about some kingdom up in Heaven; they tell us what is happening every day here on Earth. Even the descriptions of dying in the scriptures are sur-prisingly like the accounts of people who were clinically dead and then, like Lazarus, came back to life. In the transit lounge between life and death, their spirit rises out of their body, they see the scene from above, they feel drawn to a warm, diffuse light like that of a lamp which is in a niche, and, although they are unconscious, they are later able to describe what went on in the room and report the words that it is medically impossible for them to have heard. Not so differently from dreamers, whose consciousness floats from here to there, the dying lose the feeling of time, the feeling of a fixed location in space.

After I've raised the ire of the developmental psychologist, the Religious Education teacher and the car mechanic, a doctor would no doubt set me straight that Lazarus could not have had a near-death experience: after all, he had been buried for several days by the time Jesus brought him back to life. And yet medicine recognizes there is an intermediate state from which some patients miraculously return. And religion teaches that a tiny scrap of the secrets that surround us are revealed then. 'Die before you die', said the Prophet, and of course he wasn't advocating an overdose of sleeping pills or a daredevil free-climbing tour. But if you recall his first revelation, when the angel Gabriel choked him senseless, and remember the earliest Muslims' reports that he rolled on the floor, lashed out with his fists and foamed at the mouth like an epileptic, and the proph-ets before him did too – then perhaps Muhammad's saying refers to something very real: he actually did die a thousand deaths, as we say when someone is frightened to the point of panic.

In just such extreme situations, when we think we are about to lose everything, leave everything behind, or look death in the eye, we are granted a brief glimpse of metaphysics: that's Greek for 'what's beyond (or above) physics'; in other words, beyond the boundaries of the reality we can perceive through our senses. That's why doctors and nurses talk to patients who are comatose, touch them, and play them music they like. They learn this not just in the lecture hall, but in the intensive care unit. And a peace comes down, the revelations promise, and the dying who have come back to life report, and you will feel that yourself when you see someone stop breathing. It may be your father, your mother.

God takes the souls when they die,
And those that do not die, in their sleep.
But if He has decreed their death, He holds them fast;
The others He sends back for an appointed time.
Behold, therein are signs for those who reflect.

Surah 39:42

God takes the souls when they die, and also when they sleep. What does that mean? I suspect it means that, when we die, God unbinds us from time, and also every night when we dream. It means we no longer feel that what has begun must also end at the appointed time. It means that dreams are a kind of brief death in which you float through space and time. Now and again, we manage this even in waking – in play for example, in love, listening to music, daydreaming, or in special moments of bliss: by forgetting time, we cheat death. Or, no, we die before we die, and from then on we have an inkling of what is beyond our finite lives, or above our day-to-day reality. Objectively, this timelessness doesn't last long, of course – only seconds or a few minutes. Except you don't notice that yourself. Only after your thinking has started again will you say perhaps: that felt like an eternity. Or: ah! how fleeting was my joy.

A day with your Lord
Is like a thousand years
As you reckon them.

Surah 22:47

Who knows, maybe the one or at most two seconds when I thought I was skidding towards a tree were not just an image or a taste of eternity. Perhaps they were eternity itself. In any case, I can imagine that everything the religions say about the next life – that the angels take your soul, you fly up to Heaven, the Last Judgement, Paradise and Hell, life everlasting – that all that happens in the seconds or the few minutes during which you are dying.

I'll tell you another story about the Prophet. When his wife Khadija died, the Prophet fell into such deep grief that the archangel Gabriel, to take his mind off it, fetched him from Mecca and took him on a journey to Heaven. When they reached God's gate, Gabriel said he must leave Muhammad there.

'Where are we then?' Muhammad asked.

'We are where one more step would burn me', Gabriel answered.

'And what shall I do?'

'Only to you is it granted to go on.'

'But how? How? Tell me!'

'With love, O beloved of God. Take your next step with love.'

Remember, in yesterday's chapter, the ten seconds that the history of humanity takes compared with the history of all creation, the hundred kilometres of nothingness between the two grains of sand that neighbouring solar systems are? Individual human beings may feel lost, lonesome and insignificant when they look at the stars or lie on their deathbed. But it doesn't take much for them to know that they are nonetheless secure and well cared for. It only takes another person they love, or a God they know they have in their heart.

Just think how many random events led to the meeting of the two exact cells, out of trillions and trillions of possibilities, that produced you. A tiny hand movement to the left or right as I embraced your mama, a tiny cough – nonsense: a single breath, and you would have been someone completely different, a boy perhaps, an egoist, or a Monopoly genius like me. And how many random events led to your mama and me falling in love! I could have signed up for a different seminar back then at uni – I really considered it – and I never would have met her. And she, too, of course – what chance events led to us both reading the same subject at the same time in the same place? Your mama's parents and mine all independently deciding to emigrate because Iran was ruled by a dictator – and what complications of global politics had led to the country losing its freedom? Ten centimetres to the left when your grandpa fell asleep at the wheel in Austria during the long drive to Germany, and your grandparents would have died many years before I could have been born; a second later, two at the most, the car would have smashed into a tree.

And the converse is equally true, of course: I was just reading in a book about black holes – I have to keep up if I want you to take me seriously! – that extremely small changes change the future completely. Did I say a tiny cough? An ant clearing its throat has an effect on where exactly the Earth will be in its orbit more than 10 million years from now. Just imagine, an ant! And so on and so forth; it's enough to make you dizzy if you consider why everything had to happen exactly as it did happen in order for you to exist at all, and how everything will be because we exist as we do. And, every time, it brings you back to the question: why is there me, and why isn't there just nothing? And what was there before there was something? What will there be when there is nothing left?

The answers are different, just as each of the blind villagers touched a different part of the elephant, but from the beginning people have felt – grasped – that the elephant is really there, a living power that united not only your father and your mother in love, but also your grandparents, your great-grandparents, and all your ancestors in exactly the right second at exactly the right place with exactly the right breath, among so many possibilities, for you to exist. I look at you and I not only believe – I know, know it with my eyes, my ears, my heart, that you are not a fluke.

The Big Maybe

Yesterday, you asked me to say or, better yet, define once in simple words what mysticism is before we get to the end of the book. I can't just keep skirting around it, you said, with allegories, elephants, black lights, journeys to heaven . . .

All right, then, I'll try. Religions embrace all of life. They involve child-raising and spiritual guidance, worship services and feast days, supporting the poor and the orphans. They deal with how people greet one another, how people bury the dead, what is grounds for a divorce, who receives what share of an inheritance. Religions are concerned not least with what justice means in society, what responsibility means in work, what charity means in living from day to day, and so on and so forth. Thus religion consists, among other things, of a lot of practical matters. That's why the priest interpreting the Bible in the church service at your school ends up talking about refugees and climate change.

If you compare the religions' traditions, customs, rules, celebrations or doctrines, you can't expect to find many similarities. No; they are as diverse as people are, and as peoples are. For now, I'll call these things – oh God, another metaphor! – a religion's clothes.

I'm afraid we writers are not the ones to ask for definitions. We can't help speaking in images.

At the same time, however, you find in every religion the realization that God works – breathes, dwells – within human beings themselves, and the closer the different religions' believers come to their own soul, the more similar their insights and even their prayers become.

Now please don't ask me what the soul is, because then I'd have to start another book. It's easier to explain what the soul is *not*: it's *not* your everyday I, the one you mean when you say, 'I want this; I want that.' In that 'I' is the residue of your upbringing, your formative experiences, the expectations of your society, your ambitions, the needs you think of as your own although they may have been suggested by your parents, your friends or advertising – in short, everything that has influenced you since your birth, and also the upbringing, influences and experience of your ancestors. Including your and my religion. The I is the finite part of you, the temporal, personal and transitory. The eternal part of you, which you have in common with all other human beings, is called the soul. The journey to the soul is an exciting one.

This inner aspect of faith is what we call mysticism: you could say it's a religion's body – which does need clothes, though, to keep it from freezing in day-to-day living or burning up in the midday sun: a jacket to keep off the rain of so many opinions; shoes to walk over the sharp stones of egoism; sometimes glasses to see past society's prejudices. Besides, clothes adorn the body: don't underrate ornament! The beautiful, inexpedient and useless things, such as music, singing, friendly gestures, politeness: these are also important in life – vitally important. Everywhere in the world.

Take for example the differences between Islam and Hinduism: here the equality of all people; there the caste system. Take the different beliefs: here one God; there many gods. The differences could hardly be greater. And yet, in the villages where mysticism has remained strong, Hindus and Muslims revere the same saints and pray together in the temples even today.

And mysticism certainly does have to do with practical experiences – but those which occur in every life; the fundamental experiences, not the ones that are limited to a certain time, a certain place. Every person gasps for air when they can't breathe; every child longs for security; every mother loves her child; every person dies. Religions include what is changeable about human beings, yet mysticism expresses all that which always stays the same. That is why it is so similar all over the world. That is why every person encounters it.

Remember our summer hike in the Pyrenees, when we were far away from all civilization for five days, and close to the sky. True, you were talking to Louisa most of the time – not to say nonstop – and your topics, at least when I was listening, were, well, not exactly spiritual. But even you two stopped on the pass and looked out silently for minutes over the majestic landscape, the peaks all around like a cut-out silhouette, the rocky slopes covered with snow, the lakes sprinkled in the valleys, reflecting the blue of the sky; no sound to be heard, but the air cool, clear and soothing as an elixir spreading through the body . . .

. . . all right, all right, I'll stop waxing poetic.

Okay, we'll make it shorter: even you and Louisa found the Pyrenees 'lost', to use your expression. What kind of a feeling has – I won't say 'overwhelmed', you're more the reserved type – what kind of a feeling has always crept over people when they experience such natural beauty, whether in biblical times or today, whether in the Pyrenees or the Arabian desert?

Because you're at school at the moment, and my questions, as you keep complaining, are only rhetorical anyway, I'll go ahead and tell you about the feeling that overwhelmed me on a different day, a much happier one. There's no other word for it: overwhelmed, as if a higher power had seized and shaken me, thrown me down and raised me up. I mean the feeling twelve years ago when you came into the world.

You know the circumstances were dramatic; the labour pains began three months too early, and we didn't know whether you would survive. Even the doctors and nurses around us were frantic and nervous. I held your mama's hand while the nurses pushed her trolley bed at a run through an endless succession of corridors, although in reality the operating room can hardly have been more than 100 metres away. Time slowed down excruciatingly, and the corridor seemed to have no exit. But then, from one second to the next, everything went very fast: Mama was lifted onto a steel table, and the nurses put up a curtain over her chest so we wouldn't see the operation. As if in a trance, I sat down on a swivelling stool and stroked your mama's head. Then endless waiting again, supplications, comforting words in your mama's ear, and worrying that my heart pounding would betray my own apprehension. All that could be heard from the other side of the curtain were the doctor's terse, concentrated instructions, the clatter of instruments, and the peeping of the electronics.

Suddenly, the doctor's voice, almost a shout: 'Got it', more piercing than all the drums, trumpets and pipes that announce the Resurrection in the Bible. And in the next moment – although minutes must have passed before your umbilical cord had been cut and you had been cleaned and wrapped in blankets – in the next moment a nurse handed you to me.

And so I came to myself with you on my chest in front of the medical instruments that were wired to you; no one seemed interested in the two of us because your mama had to be taken care of first, and I thought, with no exaggeration, this here, exactly this, is the greatest gift that I can be given on earth. A human being has been created! Our love has created! *Kun fa-yakūn*: '"Be!" and it is.' It can't get more beautiful than this even in Heaven; nor would I go back, even into the womb. And yet, at the same time, I knew: I am standing in an operating room in Cologne University Hospital. I knew: this window-less, cold-tiled, harshly lit room, this is reality. Even now as I write this down, while you're at school being bored or having fun with science – even twelve years later, tears come to my eyes when I remember your birth. And not only that: for the moment, I am reconciled with the life we've had since then, including the sad things that have happened because of which we're no longer one family.

What did I feel? In a word: gratitude. I didn't think of God or anything like that, and I was much too busy to say a prayer. I was simply grateful that you exist and that your mama was all right. But being grateful means being grateful to someone or something. To whom?

Of course I was grateful to your mama, who had borne so much to bring you into the world; grateful to the doctors, the nurses, the machines all around measuring your heartbeat and supplying you with oxygen; grateful too to the people who had invented the machines. But that wasn't all; it was a much more all-encompassing feeling, and unattached to this or that person, this or that object. I was grateful to . . .

. . . yes, to whom? or to what? . . .

. . . to that power that had created the 1,400 grams of you. For a moment, I was grateful in every cell of my existence, and perhaps that was nothing other than being filled with God. Maybe that's why I didn't think of God: because I felt one with Him and at the same time with you; one with the Creator and the Creation.

He is the Knower
Of the hidden and the visible,
The Mighty, the Merciful,
Who made all things beautiful that He created,
And Who first created Man out of clay.
Then He made his progeny
Out of a brew of base water;

Then He shaped him
And blew of His spirit into him,
And He made for you ears, eyes, heart.
What little thanks you give!

Surah 32:6ff.

Obviously, an outside observer would have said I was just
overwrought, and of course my adrenalin was going wild. But
it always looks funny to outside observers when someone is
beside themselves, and the prophets were even pronounced ill
because they rolled on the ground flailing and foaming at the
mouth when God spoke to them (don't worry, I didn't do all
that in the delivery room, otherwise they would have taken me
up or down a few floors to the psychiatric ward). This evening,
you'll bring me back down to earth anyway: your experience of
the Pyrenees probably wasn't so sublime after all. But didn't you
too have the feeling, when you looked down at the landscape
that no artist could have ever painted more gloriously – didn't
you have the feeling that life, no matter what explanation there
might be for each individual phenomenon, is a miracle?

I know, that sounds like a greetings card again: life is a miracle. Good God.

What can I do? Truths are always the same, and have been
for about the last 6,000 years; a person can only stand there
gaping in awe. It's language that's worn out. Even we writers
often don't know any more how we can talk about the divine,
about the holiness of life, about the beauty of nature, about the
joy of love, without sounding trite. After all, the same words
pop up every day in advertising, pop songs and prime-time TV.
Just yesterday, for example, while I was googling something, I
ran across a heading that seemed to be germane to our book:
'Every action produces a reaction.' This is an absolutely true
sentence which concisely sums up the fundamental mecha-
nism of Creation; very profound – I thought. Who said it? Lao
Tse, Muhammad, Immanuel Kant? I clicked on the link and

was supplied with the 'Ten Best Weight Loss Tips': thanks a lot.

In fact, many of our truisms, proverbs and even the slogans of fitness centres, business schools and performance coaches originally came from humanity's great teachers of wisdom – nevertheless, we can't stand to hear them any more. That's more or less as if Schubert's Impromptu were the background music in every department store: that would kill even Schubert. But if you were to concoct some complicated phrase for the simple truth, that would sound wrong too. Actually, I suspect one reason why the religions have such a hard time today is because they no longer have a language: at least, no living, compelling language of their own – the old texts are still tremendous and, in all their strangeness, fresh – in which to bear witness to the heavenly event that takes place here on our little Earth with every heartbeat.

But just you wait until such a little bit of pure poetry, of Creation, comes into being before your eyes: then you won't need any priests or any imams, any commandments or principles, to fall to your knees in gratitude. In prayer, we recreate this movement with our bodies several times a day so that the rest of the time, when we're sitting in a classroom, at our desk, or stuck in traffic, when we're shopping, among friends or even visiting your grandpa's grave – so that, in day-to-day life, we never forget to give thanks. We lift our outstretched hands to the height of our head, as if we were giving attention to everything that comes into our sight, pricking up our ears or catching every puff of wind, and we speak: *allāhu akbar* – God is greater. Then we remain standing and recite the Fatiha and another surah of our choice from the Quran, and then bow deeply in praise of God. Our body still understands all this, the outdated gestures, strange movements and 1,400-year-old – and hence strange, and moreover Arabic – verses. It's best if you hear them instead of just reading them, and, if you like, you can say the Fatiha with your lips and do the movements along with me. The way I learned it from my parents when I was a child.

Bismi llāhi r-raḥmāni r-raḥīm	In the name of God, the Merciful, the Compassionate.
Al-ḥamdu li-llāhi rabbi l-ʿālamīn	Praise be to God, Lord of the worlds,
Ar-raḥmāni r-raḥīm	The Merciful, the Compassionate,
Māliki yaumi d-dīn	The King of the day of judgement.
Iyāka naʿbudu wa-iyāka nastaʿīn	Thee we serve, to Thee we pray for help.
Ihdinā ṣ-ṣirāṭa l-mustaqim	Lead us in the right path,
Ṣirāta lladīna anʿamta ʿalayhim	The path of them whom Thou hast blessed,
Ġairi l-maġḍūbi ʿalayhim	Not of them on whom your wrath lies,
Wa-lā ḍ-ḍāllīn	Nor of them who stray.

After we have devoted ourselves to the words of God, we first fall to our knees in gratitude, and then prostrate ourselves with our forehead on a little piece of dried earth – that is, a piece of nature. Then we kneel a second time and ask for forgiveness before we rise and stand upright again with our chest wide. We repeat this several times, and, if you want, you can stay a while at the end listening inside you, or telling God your wishes and intentions. We end the prayers with a greeting to our right and to our left, no matter who is kneeling next to us in the mosque, or whether we are alone: *As-salāmu ʿalaykum wa-raḥmatu llāh* – 'Peace be with you and God's mercy.' Thus the last sentence of the prayer – and this is important – is for our fellow human beings. Then, when we stand up, we go on with our day-to-day life in the knowledge that God's mercy flows in us with every breath.

And what, I sometimes wonder, what if you had been still-born? Would I still have been grateful?

Hardly.

And would I tell a torture victim, a starving child, a raped woman, a family whose livelihood has been destroyed in war, or a refugee to whom we give no refuge – would I still assure such an innocent sufferer that the world is 'the breath of the Merciful'?

I don't think so.

Nevertheless, the hungry, the disadvantaged, the maltreated, the forlorn also speak to God, and often more than the fortunate. Why is that?

Let me go back once more to your birth – when it was still uncertain whether you would survive. I asked, I pleaded, I begged for everything to come out all right. But asking, pleading, begging means addressing someone or something. Whom? That same power that could just as well have taken you back to itself before you were even born. I believe that is what's meant, or part of what's meant, when the Quran says every human being surrenders to God from birth: from their very first breath, human beings address something that they cannot even describe, let alone understand; questioningly with their first scream, somewhat more calmly with the first caress, then later pleadingly in their need and, we hope, gratefully in their happiness. And when it literally left me speechless – when I was 'lost', to use your term again, which is altogether fitting – all I had left was prayer; that is, sentences that said themselves, formed by the lips of countless people and learned by heart in my childhood. They gave me strength, they gave me courage, they brought back the confidence that your mama needed, the confidence that everything would turn out all right, even though I had long since learned from experience that some things, many things, turn out badly, and God does not grant all prayers.

God burdens no soul with more than it can carry.
What it has earned is in its favour,

What it has deserved is against it.
'Our Lord! Do not reprove us
If we forget or err!
Our Lord! Do not burden us
As you burdened those who were before us!
Our Lord! Do not burden us beyond our strength!
Forgive us, absolve us, and have mercy on us!'

Surah 2:286

If I remember correctly, I didn't pray because I believed; it was the other way around: I believed in God because in prayer I instinctively addressed that which creates life and takes it away again. I looked towards it; it was there in the room, in the fluorescent tubes and their cold light; in the doctor's fingers that I pictured on the other side of the curtain; in your mother who was giving you birth; as palpable as a puff of cool air or a surge of heat; as loud as my own heart pounding; as menacing as death and as glorious as the 1,400 grams when I pressed you to my chest. Call it what you will; call it omnipotence or end-lessness, the creative principle, the ground of all being; the soul of the world or the holy spirit; love, emptiness or the breath of compassion. Many people call it God.

But again: what if you hadn't started breathing, opened your mouth, your eyes, your ears, your heart? Surely I would have lamented, and maybe I would have complained against God. Accusation too is a relationship that the religions tell of. People who denounce God believe in Him too.

Have you ever heard of Job? Probably not in your Religious Education lessons.

Job was the most righteous of his people, and yet every-thing was taken from him: his house, his wife, his children, his reputation, his health, his fortune, even his clothes. One plague after another struck him until he found himself naked on a dungheap, his skin covered with terrible sores, everyone taunting him and even throwing muck at him. All that was left of his possessions was a piece of broken glass that he used to scratch himself – the most loving, god-fearing person on Earth. Finally, he couldn't contain himself any more, and he shouted out all his rage against God. And still Job is a prophet in Islam:

> What an excellent servant he was.
> Behold, he was penitent.
>
> *Surah 38:44*

Job was not at all penitent, and the Muslims knew it. Job had rebelled against God: 'Know now that God hath overthrown me,' he complained; 'Behold, I cry out of wrong, but I am not heard: I cry aloud, but there is no judgement.' These and many other heretical statements are not found in the Quran; they are in the biblical story of Job, which was well known to Muhammad's listeners. But the Quran does not deny Job's rebellion; it simply passes over it in silence:

> And Job,
> When he called to his Lord,
> 'Affliction has come upon me,
> Yet Thou art the most merciful of the merciful.'
>
> *Surah 21:83*

Yes, in the Bible too, Job found his way back to God; God forgave him and rewarded him richly. That is what the Quran alludes to here. And yet Job hadn't retracted any part of his denunciation, neither in the Bible nor in the Quran, and in Islamic literature his complaint has been retold time after time. He became a prophet, accusation and all. This is the example that the Quran calls to mind: not even in the worst distress imaginable did Job turn his face away from God. By denouncing God, he sued for God's justice. He loved as only a person who feels abandoned can love.

Say: 'To whom belongs what is in the Heavens and on Earth?'
Say: 'To God!'
He has committed Himself to mercy.
He will gather you on the Day of Resurrection,
There is no doubt of it.
But those who have lost themselves, they do not believe.

Surah 6:12

Do you know what my favourite word in the Quran is? The word 'maybe'. There are few words that occur more often in the Quran; you have also heard it often in our evening talks on religion. In Arabic: *la'alla*. Maybe you will be grateful; maybe you will understand; maybe you will realize; maybe you will come to your senses; maybe you will return; maybe you will find mercy. That means it is also possible that you *won't* understand God; maybe you will be angry with Him or deny Him. This 'maybe' contains your freedom, your responsibility, your search for knowledge. But this 'maybe' contains still more. The whole drama that is Creation, and has been since the first cell division, is contained in this 'maybe'. You might not have been born. No one had to be born. Your grandpa wanted only one word on his tombstone: *shokr* – thanks.

Epilogue

Last night you said what I had written sounded quite reasonable, on the whole – but how should you know if it's true? It's hard to imagine, you said, some kind of good power out there somewhere, or inside us either for that matter, that created the world. No, you said, you're not yet convinced. And you still don't really understand who or what God actually is, you said.

That is painful for me to hear, of course, and I'm afraid I haven't fulfilled your grandpa's request very well. Be that as it may, though, I doubted God too at your age, and even today I wouldn't say I find everything my parents taught me about Islam is true, or that I have found it all confirmed in the course of life. And your grandpa in turn certainly didn't accept everything his parents had taught him – your great-grandparents, who lived in a world completely different from the one you live in: born in the nineteenth century in Iran, when there wasn't even electricity or running water; no machines; hardly any of our contemporary ideas. Your grandpa travelled far, emigrated, sought his own path, together with your grandma; a path that was not nearly as straight as the one God recommends in the Fatiha, and the one parents recommend to their child. Your grandpa did indeed stray; he said so himself; and for most of his life he was not as devout as when you knew him.

I can't spend every evening explaining that God is not a rational matter, God can only be experienced – and then expect you to be convinced by words alone. But what then?

Recently, I asked a friend how he taught religion to his children, and my friend answered: through practice. His children went to church from an early age, and, long before they could understand much, they had experienced the atmosphere, the singing, the organ music, the ceremonial vestments of the priests and acolytes, the aromas, the genuflections, the melodious prayers, the very special reverence during the Eucharist, the offertory, the symbolic embrace with neighbours in the pews at the end of the Mass, no matter how old or young, whether poor or rich. The Advent season before every Christmas; the fasting after Carnival; Easter, the Ascension, Pentecost – all year long, not just the calendar of school holidays, but at the same time a celestial calendar. Later, his children became altar servers themselves, learned the rosary, joined the Boy Scouts, experienced the communal aspects of their religion, aiding the homeless and collecting donations in the pedestrian zone. Of course, his children had also attended Religious Education in school and studied the Catechism. But the crucial thing was practice, my friend said, in the sense of practising something to learn it, like practising the piano. The brain turns away from God and comes back again, sometimes in one direction, sometimes in the other; this is the same with his children, he says, who are adults by now. No rational person is free of doubt; everyone has to deal with it in their own way. But the body, the disposition, they don't forget their trust in God, and sometime in the course of life, faith turns up again.

What my friend said made me thoughtful, and a little bit sad, too. In Germany, you have no religious community, no mosque, no congregational life. Other Muslims may have them, but we Iranians don't. After all, most of us fled from the religion that has ruled in our country since the revolution, or are the children and grandchildren of refugees and exiles. The only practice I had to offer you, besides my own clumsy exercises, was that of your grandparents, who grew up with the religious calendar, and now your grandpa is dead. We Muslims in Europe are in a strange land, in exile. But even if we lived in Iran, it wouldn't be so very different: I don't see anyone among my relatives and friends of my own age or younger who still practises Islam – really, not one. Since the Islamic revolution, some Iranians even have a regular loathing of the religion, much more so than the people in Europe. In Europe, the religion is met more with indifference and ignorance. In Iran, it's much worse, at least in our circles: many people hate religion, and no wonder, when torture and murder are being committed in its name. With my religiousness, I would be foreign in Iran too – especially in Iran.

My friend told me, though, that it's not so very different in Europe. Everywhere in the modern, high-tech world, religion is in retreat, and when large numbers of people claim to be returning to faith today, they are usually turning to movements that are openly opposed to their own traditions, in Christianity as elsewhere. In South America, for example, in deeply Catholic South America, the Catholics will soon be in the minority because, year after year, millions of Christians are switching to new churches, usually fundamentalist ones – Europeans haven't really realized this yet. And not even my friend's own Catholic Church retains its respect for the mystery of language, the truth of images, and the beauty of service. But instead of being sad, he often thinks: the early Christians were also a minority, and they lived their faith all the more persuasively for that. Maybe – maybe! – in foreignness, in weakness, in poverty there is also a strength, and conversely in power, in majority, in wealth, there is a danger. Power tempts people to abuse it; majority tempts people to self-righteousness, wealth tempts people to greed; that is true not only in Iran, my friend said; it has also happened often enough in the history of Christianity.

I'm not sure whether my friend is right. As I child I didn't have a congregation, a mosque or Muslim friends any more than you have. And yet, as your father, I'm teaching you Islam as well as I can. When I consider how I found faith, I can't think of anything I practised like the piano. In my case, it was the believers themselves: first of all my parents, of course, then my aunts and uncles and my own grandparents in Iran. They were very kind people, and they were very devout people, and so my childish mind made kindness and devoutness synonymous.

Later, I learned that believers are not always better people by any means, but often quite the opposite. And yet I encountered again and again, on all my travels, in every country, a love that seemed to be grounded not just in this world, but in people's trust in God. Because that love didn't want anything back.

No, I am not sure whether my friend is right, he who practised faith with his children like a serious and gracious game – whether the people who give an example of kindness and devoutness are not more important, no matter what the religion. Nevertheless, I will give you his idea, the idea of a Christian, as the closing thought of my book. Because now you are turning the pages on which you will ask your own questions. God willing, you will gather experience and learn so much more, you will fall in love and sometimes be disappointed, you will travel, choose a profession and start a family; you will fall ill but then get well again, you will miss your children when they have left home, you will bury your parents, tell your grandchildren stories, grow frail, and finally die yourself. You will remember your grandpa, the charity he founded for the poor, his joy when he looked at the sea in Spain, his patience in his sickness, his lost look between all the machines in the intensive care unit, his serenity even on his deathbed, because death to him was a second trip, and the more important one, through the birth canal. You will remember our talks and know at least one, two prayers by heart, no matter whether you believe in God or not. Maybe – maybe! – someday the prayers will speak themselves.

How This Book Came to Be

When I am writing, there are usually many books on my desk, and I read in them or leaf through them. In working on the present book, however, my desk remained bare at first, except for the sources I have quoted. To strike the right tone and to permit myself all the simplifications, exaggerations and overly broad strokes through the history of the world religions that were necessary for my project, I began by drawing exclusively on what has stayed with me from my readings and what sprouted in my own thoughts. Thus, there are many other books in this book, although I hardly know which ones. Likewise, several anecdotes from my earlier books reappear. The most important source, however, was my religious upbringing and the example of my parents, older relatives and teachers.

Only in a later phase of work did I refer to the scholarly literature to check my manuscript and to fill in the gaps. On the Quran, that literature included the studies of Nasr Hamid Abu Zayd, Kenneth Cragg, Toshihiko Izutsu, Angelika Neuwirth, Frithjof Schuon and Michael Seils. On Sufism and Ibn Arabi in particular, I relied mainly on the works of Claude Addas, Titus Burckhardt, William C. Chittick, Michel Chodkiewicz,

Henry Corbin, Stephen Hirtenstein, Annemarie Schimmel and Sa'diyya Shaikh. Again and again, I referred to Jack Miles's two books on the Bible and the Quran, and to a book by Gert von Natzmer which is out of print, sadly: *Auf der Suche nach dem Sinn: Religionen und Weltanschauungen* [The search for meaning: religions and ideologies] (Munich and Berlin, 1980). I am indebted to the latter for the distinction between cyclical and linear time, and for the translation of the age and extent of the universe to earthly dimensions. On my forays into physics, I followed Niels Bohr, Hans-Peter Dürr, Arthur Eddington, Albert Einstein, Heino Falcke, Werner Heisenberg, Christine and Frido Mann, Max Planck, Carlo Rovelli, Erwin Schrödinger and Guido Tonelli. I read about the astronauts' impressions in Frank White.

The translations from the Quran are my own. In writing them, I often drew on Hartmut Bobzin, Max Henning, Friedrich Rückert, whose translations are correct, each in its own way, and certainly often better than my own. For the present book, I had to find a diction that is easily understandable to younger readers and listeners, without entirely losing the strange and enigmatic quality of the original. This English edition also draws on the translations of Arthur J. Arberry, M. M. Pickthall and M. A. S. Abdel Haleem.

The Protestant theologian Friedrich Wilhelm Graf, Munich, and my doctoral advisor, the Arabist Stefan Wild, Bonn, read the first draft of my manuscript and saved me from several mistakes. They also gave me many of their own insights, which I included in the second draft. This draft was corrected by the Islamic theologians Bekim Agai, Frankfurt, and Muna Tatari, Paderborn, who made many helpful comments. I have long carried on a conversation about religion, and hence about the manuscript of the present book, with my friends Carl Hegemann, Martin Mosebach and Stefan Otteni. Finally, I have had extremely critical listeners in my own children and in their friends Mathilde, Carlotta and Nico.

My editor was Carolin Mandel; Georg Oswald of Carl Hanser Verlag also read the manuscript. The academic editor was the theologian Klaus von Stosch, Bonn. The astrophysicist and philosopher Sibylle Anderl, Frankfurt, commented on the scientific passages.

Nonetheless, I am responsible for those errors that remain, especially as I sometimes stubbornly ignored the advice of my editors and first readers. I am most deeply grateful to every one of them.